THE EMPOWERED TEACHER TOOLKIT

Proven Strategies to Take Control of Your
Time, Your Energy & Your Passion for Teaching

GRACE STEVENS

Red Lotus Books

Contents

Prologue	1
1. AN AWKWARD BEGINNING	3
Who Will Love This Book	7
How To Use This Book	9
My Promise to You	10
2. ECHO FRAMEWORK FOR EDUCATOR EMPOWERMENT	11
3. FOLLOW YOUR NORTH STAR	16
Be Versus Do	19
The Revolutionary Behind the Door	24
Summary	28
Get Empowered:	28
Ways To Practice This Mindset Habit Starting Today	28
4. SEPARATE YOUR WORTH FROM YOUR WORK	30
Summary	38
Get Empowered!	38
Ways To Practice This Mindset Habit Starting Today	38
5. FOCUS ON WHAT YOU CAN CONTROL	42
The Accidental Path	42
Applying This in the Classroom	47
Completing the Exercise - Concerns v. Control	49
Proactive versus Reactive	55
Dealing With Student Trauma	58
Summary	63
Get Empowered	63
Ways To Practice This Mindset Habit Starting Today	63
6. REDEFINE BALANCE	67
Glass Versus Rubber Balls	69
Urgent and Important Are Not the Same Thing	77
The Decision Matrix	79

Wheel of School/Life Balance	82
Chapter Summary	94
Get Empowered	94
Wys To Practice This Mindset Habit Starting Today	94
7. PERFECT THE ART OF SAYING "NO" IN A SCHOOL SETTING	97
A Crash Course in Saying "No"	98
Saying "Yes" With Limitations	102
Chapter Summary	105
Get Empowered	105
Ways to Practice This Mindset Habit Starting Today	105
8. BE INTENTIONAL ABOUT YOUR NARRATIVE	107
Examining Your Teaching Story	108
Retune Your Satellite Radio	111
Becoming Aware of Your Story	114
Stick with the Facts	120
Chapter Summary	125
Get Empowered	125
Ways To Practice This Mindset Habit Starting Today	125
9. PROACTIVELY PROTECT YOUR PEACE	127
Unsubscribe From the Drama	129
When the Drama is a Teammate	132
It's Not a Competition	134
Go on a Mental Diet Detox	135
A Quick Word About the News Cycle	138
Summary	139
Get Empowered	139
Ways to Practice This Mindset Habit Starting Today	139
10. COMING FULL CIRCLE	142
Here's Your Essential Roadmap:	143
Gently Now - Setting Yourself Up for Success	144
Epilogue	148

Good Karma Request	151
Need More?	153
About the Author	155
Also by Grace Stevens	157

Copyright © 2024 by Grace Stevens

Published by Red Lotus Books

Grace Stevens LLC

Cover design: @kingof_designer

ISBN: 978-0-9987019-9-8

No part of this book may be reproduced in any form or by any electronic or mechanical means, including information storage and retrieval systems, without written permission from the author, except for the use of brief quotations in a book review.

This includes all exercises and information in the Companion Workbook.

Disclaimer

This book offers information and is designed for educational purposes only. This information is not a substitute for, nor does it replace professional medical advice, diagnosis, or treatment. The author and publisher shall have neither liability nor responsibility to any person or entity with respect to any loss or damage caused or alleged to be caused directly or indirectly by this book.

em·pow·er

/imˈpouər/

make (someone) stronger and more confident, especially in controlling their life and claiming their rights

E·VOLVE

/əˈvôlv,əˈvälv/

develop gradually, especially from a simple to a more complex form, in order to improve the likelihood of survival

TOOL·KIT

/tool kit/

a personal set of resources, abilities, or skills

OXFORD ENGLISH DICTIONARY (2024)

IMPORTANT:

To get the maximum benefit from this book, please download the Companion Workbook by visiting

www.gracestevens.com/empowerbook

1

An Awkward Beginning

The challenge with writing a book for teachers is this nagging insecurity that my readers are scanning it for grammatical and structural errors and that it will get handed back to me with red pen bleeding in all the margins. If I were grading this book, I know that my comment would be something along the lines of, "Excellent and relevant content, but the introduction needs a lot of work." The comment would be in purple pen because I once read that writing in red ink could be culturally offensive.

This introduction is probably not the most compelling piece of literature you have ever read. Over the last six years, this book has had five different introductions and even more variations of titles. My favorite was *"Take Control of Your Teacher Life: Strategies for Teachers Who Are Overworked, Overwhelmed, and Over It!"* I argued it contained your basic "rule of three," alliteration and was straight to the point. My editors, however, had concerns about the *tone*. I am known for my "positive mindset habits," and they argued the title was a little off-brand.

The book's principles and content have remained unchanged in the six years I have worked on it. What has changed is the urgency with which I need to convey them.

I have decided to stop second-guessing myself and striving for perfection and hit publish anyway. So forgive me the rocky start, and let me tell you why you should read this book if you are involved in education.

First, let's start with what you know. While teaching has never been the easiest profession, the challenges are only getting more significant. Six years ago, when I published *Positive Mindset Habits for Teachers*, the first chapter was entitled "The Elephant in the Classroom." The "elephant" no one talked about was how overwhelmed, stressed, and unhappy many educators were in their chosen field. I boldly suggested that the best thing educators could do for themselves, their students, their academic metrics, and education in general, was to prioritize putting the balance and joy back in their classrooms and their lives.

At that time, this concept was not openly expressed in educational circles. One global pandemic later, the fact that teachers are burning out, exiting the profession in droves with not nearly enough new teachers to replace them is no longer an "elephant" in the room; it's a crisis. No school district is immune from teacher and substitute teacher shortages, and new businesses have emerged dedicated to helping teachers "transition" out of education. The collective narrative around teaching has become increasingly negative and hopeless.

All of us who taught before, during, and after the pandemic know that classrooms today are fundamentally different. Students' behavior and engagement are different. Parents are different. The ever-increasing demands on teachers are different. On our worst days, meeting all those demands can feel impossible, as if we are set up to fail.

There is no quick or easy fix to the challenges in education. This much we know for sure.

However, here's the part of the situation you may still be optimistically trying to ignore: **no one is coming to save us.**

If we want to continue impacting young lives without burning out and sacrificing not just our personal lives but also our emotional, mental, and physical health, then we are going to need to evolve into a new breed of educator, one who takes responsibility for being empowered and creating our own path to success within the current system.

The need for a new skill set and tools in our toolbox has emerged —skills not taught in teacher training colleges or professional development days. These skills include setting and communicating healthy boundaries, fostering resilience, and proactively protecting our peace from negative people and narratives. We need practical strategies for becoming comfortable leaving not just our laptops and ungraded papers at school but also teacher guilt, stress, and vicarious student trauma behind.

We need to understand that no perfect teacher planner or chatGPT prompt can help us do less and leave work on time if we don't first master the skills to advocate for ourselves. We need the confidence to no longer fear the judgment of our peers if we stop volunteering for a ridiculous amount of extra duties and are no longer the last car to leave campus every night.

So, even though it is an awkward start, I am moving beyond the standard trope of starting a book with an inspiring quote or story. Instead, I begin with a plea: Evolve and learn these skills or risk turning the career you worked so hard to obtain into a stressful, overwhelming, joyless jail sentence—one where you are just trying to make it to the weekend, the next break, or early retirement.

You deserve better.

Your students deserve better.

If we don't start feeling empowered to take back control of our time and energy, focus on the things we can influence, and view teaching as a challenging adventure where we can still thrive professionally and personally, teaching may go the way of the dinosaurs. Sure, not everyone will burn out and leave. Plenty will burn out and stay. Those still loving their jobs (most days) will be left to ponder which scenario is potentially worse for education.

LET ME BE VERY CLEAR. I AM NOT IMPLYING THAT THE ISSUES IN education are your fault. Any system that is held together with duct tape and the expectation that its workers will self-sacrifice to keep it afloat needs to evolve. There are complex systemic issues at play. Let's get to the good news: **it doesn't need to be this way.**

Not every day in the classroom is magical, but plenty of educators are still excited about their role. They have many days where fun, creativity, and connection go hand in hand with learning. There are campuses where students, test scores, and teachers thrive; these things do not need to be mutually exclusive. I was one of these teachers for the better part of twenty years.

While some factors, such as resources and socio-economic backgrounds, will always make some teaching conditions more challenging than others, we have way more control over our day-to-day situation than we believe. There is a proven framework we can follow and skills we can learn that can help us be more empowered to regain balance in our lives and create a more positive experience for ourselves. This book is an excellent place to start.

Who Will Love This Book

This book is not just for teachers and will benefit anyone involved in education. While many of the scenarios and " Get Empowered"suggestions at the end of each chapter are classroom-based, the mindsets and skills will be invaluable if you are an administrator, counselor, Speech and Language Pathologist, curriculum coach, paraprofessional, or district office employee. We are all overworked and tasked with changing the collective narrative and culture around education. These are the exact "resources, abilities, and skills" we all need in our toolbox.

You will find this information helpful and empowering if any of the following resonate:

- YOU ARE FRUSTRATED BY HOW MANY HOURS YOU WORK. YOU ARE tired that everything and everyone else in your life seems to come second to the demands of your job. Your family complains about how many hours you work.

- YOU WANT TO LEAVE WORK AT SCHOOL, NOT JUST PHYSICALLY BUT emotionally. You are tired of the stress and mental and emotional toll teaching takes on you, robbing you of your sleep and your health. Even when you are not at school, you constantly worry and are not fully present in other areas of your life.

- YOU KNOW YOU NEED MORE BALANCE BUT DON'T KNOW WHERE TO start setting boundaries and priorities. You are concerned that if you do, you will be judged as selfish, not a team player, and not caring enough about your students. You are tired of feeling coerced into extra duties that have nothing to do with your primary role or your interests.

- YOU FEEL OBLIGED TO ACCOMMODATE REQUESTS FROM PARENTS, administrators, students, and even co-workers that are often unreasonable and well beyond the terms of your contract. You comply, but you are increasingly resentful despite smiling when you agree.

- YOU ARE STARTING TO WORRY THAT A CAREER IN EDUCATION IS not sustainable. You were so excited to become a teacher, but now you are on the road to burnout and know you can't keep up with this pace for the long haul. You long to reconnect to the passion you once had for teaching and students.

- YOU ARE OVERWORKED, OVERWHELMED, AND OVER IT. (I WAS determined to get that in, wasn't I?)

- YOU ARE TIRED OF GENERIC ADVICE SUCH AS "SET HEALTHIER boundaries" and "remember your why." You want a proven framework and step-by-step actions specific to a school setting given to you by someone whose in-class experience is **realistic, recent, and relevant.**

How To Use This Book

The habits, mindsets, and strategies in this book are proven and founded in science, my own experience, and the experiences of other educators I have coached. Mastering many of these skills took me years, but I want this book to be your shortcut. I promise you that if I can learn them, you can too! I would like to say that I spent twenty years studying positive psychology, cognitive behavioral therapy, and neuroscience, so you don't have to. I took twenty-plus years of nerdy study and trial and error on my behalf and turned them into a practical toolkit for you. These concepts build on each other, but if there is a particular area you feel would bring you the most immediate benefit, feel free to read the chapters out of order. Grab the tool you think you need the most!

One thing I know for sure is that knowledge without action is not particularly helpful. For that reason, at the end of every chapter, I have included specific recommendations and ways that you can integrate and apply these new skills. The Companion Workbook also contains specific exercises to help you gain clarity.

Because your success is important to me, I provide a PDF version of the Companion Workbook at no extra charge. To get access to the workbook, please visit

www.gracestevens.com/empowerbook

Of course, you could read the book without completing the exercise or using the other resources. But I'll compare the process of learning these new skills to learning anything else: if you truly want transformation, you need to get involved. It's no different than wanting to learn yoga or how to build a table. Sure, you can watch the videos and read the books, but to experience change, you will have to get on the floor or open your toolbox.

My Promise to You

Because this book is written by a teacher for teachers, I promise it is free of "edutalk" or jargon. It will be easy to read and apply. I'm not concerned with sounding academically impressive; I'm concerned with getting you results. It's short by design.

It might be a surprise to you to find a book in the educational field that makes no reference to pedagogy or student outcomes or student experience. That's because my goal is not professional development (we all sit through plenty of that) but personal growth and empowerment, specifically for educators. It focuses on helping **you** thrive. I want to help you feel empowered to take back control of your time so that you can enjoy teaching for the long haul and have the energy to show up in all areas of your life less stressed. Ironically, a less stressed, more energized, and empowered teacher is precisely what students need to succeed. Since I already dedicated over two decades to helping students, my attention is turned to you. If you want your experience to improve, I'm here for you. I promise that what I share in this book will help.

2

ECHO Framework for Educator Empowerment

First things first.

Before exploring the tools in your teacher empowerment toolbox, a basic overview of my ECHO Framework for Educator Empowerment will be helpful. I have been writing and talking about teaching for a long time; everything I cover falls into one of these four areas. As with most concepts in personal development, these areas are interrelated, but I organized them into an overarching framework for clarity.

I named it the ECHO Framework because it's easy to remember and also because we do so love acronyms in education. The term echo serves as a positive reminder that what we put out into the world is returning to us.

Here's a synopsis.

E STANDS FOR "YOUR ENERGY TEACHES MORE THAN YOUR LESSON **plans**."

. . .

IN SHORT, HOW YOU SHOW UP MATTERS. I'M NOT TALKING ABOUT the amount of physical energy you have (although being exhausted and emotionally drained makes for a tough day in the classroom.) I'm talking about your vibe. I try to avoid that word (it can come off as more crystal gazer than researcher), and if you think of a better one to describe this, please let me know. But here's what I mean by vibe: the combination of your mindset, your demeanor, your dominant thoughts, perceptions, and words. The "feeling" you give off. I could go into long explanations of resonance and neuroscience and how your energy affects others, but let's keep it simple.

Take a minute to do this now. Think back to your favorite teacher from school. Go on, take a minute. Close your eyes and put yourself back in that classroom. Stay there for a minute or two. Make the memory as visceral as possible. What made that experience so memorable?

Was it the physical elements of the classroom? Was it the grading rubrics and the textbooks?

Or was it how your favorite teacher made you feel? Were you able to sense they were in control of their emotions and the class while also conveying their passion for the subject and their faith in your ability to learn and succeed? Did you hear encouragement and laughter in that class? Did students feel safe to take risks learning or being creative? Was collaboration valued more than competition and test scores?

Now ask yourself this: how was their "vibe" different from your least favorite teacher?

Point made. It was never about the lesson plans.

. . .

C STANDS FOR "CONTROL WHAT YOU CAN CONTROL."

This concept is the foundation of empowerment, and you will find an entire section of this book dedicated to it.

H STANDS FOR "HAPPINESS CAN BE SYNTHESIZED."

The idea is that you don't have to be a victim of your circumstances or the "happiness" genes you were born with. Instead, you can intentionally adopt habits and mindsets to raise your natural happiness "set point" and create a more joyful life.

In my book *Positive Mindset Habits for Teachers*, I dive into the science of positive mindsets and "happy habits" and how to apply them in your daily life as an educator. That is also where you'll find more in-depth information on how your energy impacts your students even more than your lesson plans and why happier teachers are essential to creating productive learning environments.

You don't need to have read *Positive Mindset Habits for Teachers* to benefit from this book, but the two make an excellent pair. Maybe you picked up this book with "survival" in mind rather than "happiness," but trust me, the two are deeply connected.

O STANDS FOR "OTHER PEOPLE'S EXPERIENCE DOESN'T NEED TO BE **your experience."**

That's the essential point right there, isn't it? Many people in education are overworked, stressed, anxious, and burning out. They are sacrificing their mental, emotional, and physical health because they think that's the way it needs to be. But there is another way. Their experience doesn't need to be your experience. My goal with all my work is to empower educators with the tools necessary to create their own experiences inside and outside the classroom.

You can see that none of these four concepts function in isolation. For example, to have your own teaching experience, you need to believe that happiness is not automatically predetermined by the class list or grade assignment you just received, and you need to focus on controlling what you can control. Because the concepts are interdependent, I often present the framework as interlocking puzzle pieces.

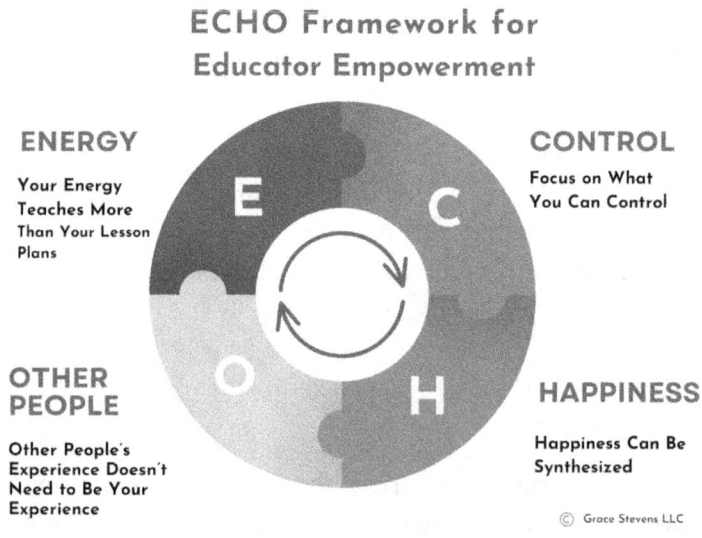

A full-size PDF you can print out as a reminder can be found in the Companion Workbook. One more time, you can access it free of charge by going to **www.gracestevens.com/empowerbook**

Enough of the preamble. You came here for practical solutions, not flow charts.

Let's dive in!

3

Follow Your North Star

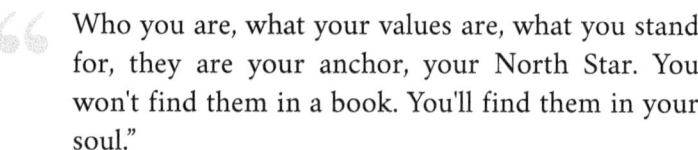 Who you are, what your values are, what you stand for, they are your anchor, your North Star. You won't find them in a book. You'll find them in your soul."

- Anne Mulcahy, Former CEO of Xerox Corp.

THIS SCENARIO PROBABLY SOUNDS FAMILIAR. IT'S THE BEGINNING OF the school year; we have a million things you could be doing in our classroom to be ready for students. Instead, we are sitting in a mandatory professional development day. Before we dive into the "critical learning," the icebreaker activity asks us to share our "why" for teaching. Cue the eye roll. With so many other priorities, it's frustrating to be asked to overshare about why we felt compelled to spend years of study and thousands of dollars of student debt to pursue a career that, on any given day, has the potential to traumatize us. We all know why we're here. It's certainly not for the fame and the glory or the free bagels. What we really want to know is, how long has that cream cheese been sitting out?

For me, my "why" is to positively impact students, influence the future, touch young minds and hearts, and pay it forward to a public school system and teachers who showed me my value, helped me believe in myself, and encouraged me to continue my education.

I was the first person in my immediate family to go to college. It was my 11th-grade drama teacher who introduced me to the possibility of higher education. It was she who procured the university application forms and helped me complete them. This was back in the 1980s, long before online applications. I went on to study in four different countries, using three different languages. All this from a kid who came from a home environment where no one could help her with homework or push her to dream a bigger dream for her life. Free public education for the win!

See, I overshared.

This is fair game in a book where it's just you and I, where you choose to spend time reading this book, and you can skip ahead if you want. It's not so great when you are trapped in a room of people, most of whom would prefer not to share, and where the answer to the question should be blatantly obvious.

We get into teaching because we love kids; we want to be a source of positivity in their lives. We want a career with purpose and impact. Sure, there may be a few teachers out there whose primary motivation was to be done by 3 PM and have summers off. But it doesn't take long to realize that there are easier ways to make money and gain respect. Any teacher who isn't genuinely passionate about teaching and thinks it will be an easy ride will become quickly disillusioned and burned out and won't last long.

Your "North Star" is not your "why" of teaching.

It's also not a mission statement.

I REMEMBER BEING CAUGHT OFF GUARD BY SOMETHING THAT looked like a ransom note on the back of the door in the women's bathroom at my most recent school. I tried all three bathrooms on campus, and they all had the same thing. A large piece of colored paper with typed sentences, different sizes, and fonts, cut out and glued on the page. Seriously, it's just like a ransom note. When I read it, I was surprised that it was our school mission statement. It read,

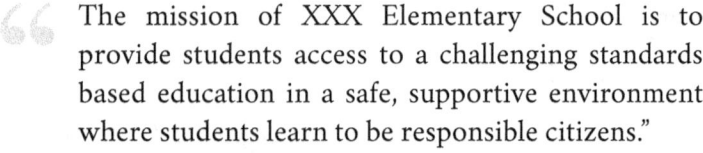

> The mission of XXX Elementary School is to provide students access to a challenging standards based education in a safe, supportive environment where students learn to be responsible citizens."

THAT MISSION STATEMENT FEELS PRETTY GENERIC AND STERILE. It doesn't do much to inspire me to hop out of bed in the morning and get busy. Or, because of its placement, hurry up in the bathroom and get back to my class because that "challenging standards-based curriculum" is waiting.

When I asked a colleague about this strange document, they explained that it looked that way because it had been part of an activity in professional development several years before. A list was made of the "kind of things that go in mission statements," and teachers voted on what they felt was important. Each group had cut out the appropriate lines that were voted on and made the mini-poster. That explained why it looked like a ransom note but not why it had been relegated to the bathrooms.

I asked the colleague if they remembered what it said, and they said, "Something about curriculum. But I remember voting to have something about school being a safe place in there."

THERE'S NOTHING WRONG PER SE WITH SCHOOL AND COMPANY mission statements. But often, they become generic documents resulting from group collaboration or negotiation. They have a "Let's just get this done because we need something on our wall and website" vibe, don't feel personal, and don't always have everyone's buy-in.

I'm guessing this activity was a check-off item on some district-wide list of mandatory documents. Does your school have a cell phone policy? Check. A safety binder? Check. A mission statement? Darn! Let's add it to the back-to-school professional development day.

Be Versus Do

Your North Star is something different. You can call it your personal mission statement. But I always remember my days of introducing the North Star to my students back in our digital star lab. The star lab was a vast dome we'd crawl into where I could project a computer-generated planetarium. It was super cool, right? I would use it to explain the movement of the constellations across the night sky. I could speed up the movement of the stars until the constellation rotated at a dizzying pace, and amidst all of the laughter and wonder, someone would always notice that one star never moved as others swirled around it—the North Star.

My North Star is what I know to be true about my teaching. It defines what I want students to experience in my classroom. It's my compass. It defines my values. And having a keen awareness of our values is essential. Few things in life cause as much stress as being pressured to act in ways that don't support them.

IN EDUCATION, WHERE THINGS CONSTANTLY CHANGE, THERE IS SO much external static competing for our attention and pulling it away from our students and what they truly need. Defining my North Star helped me feel empowered, and feel at peace when prioritizing tasks. It is a constant like that fixed star in my digital night sky. It helps guide me when things are swirling around, I am overwhelmed or have lost my way.

This is important. My North Star is not about what I want to do but about who I want to be. How do I want to show up for my students? How do I want them to feel? What do I believe is true about teaching and what students need?

THIS TIES IN WITH MY ECHO FRAMEWORK AND THE ASSERTION, *"Your energy teaches more than your lesson plans."*

Our students need us to bring our best selves to the classroom as much as possible. Teachers who are exhausted, resentful, and easily triggered by student behavior do not make for a fun, peaceful, or productive day of learning.

. . .

My North Star truths are not pinned up in my classroom. I made them into a personal mandala picture that I laminated and kept in my drawer. My mantra is in the middle of the mandala, "Teach Only Love." I usually shove it into a random place in lesson plan book. It feels like I always stumble on it at just the right moment. Personal mandalas and mantras may not appeal to you. Call it a personal mission statement if that feels more comfortable. But the point is, it's for you. It's not some sort of teaching manifesto you share with others.

Your North Star/Mandala will likely look different from mine. It doesn't need to be fancy; you can simply scribble it on a sticky note. How you write your teaching truths and remind yourself about them is irrelevant. What is important is taking the time to define them for yourself. Just keep them out of the public bathroom, please.

Here are my defining values when it comes to students and what I want them to feel in my class:

- I see you

- You matter

- You are safe here

- I believe you can achieve at a high level

- Your success is important to me

Here are my defining values when it comes to teaching:

- My energy teaches more than my lesson plans

- Connection before curriculum

- Teach only love (my mantra as a parent, teacher, coach, and general all-around human being)

The exercise in the Companion Workbook will help guide you (blank examples follow). Even if you are new to teaching, your experience as a student can help you. There is no need to overthink your answers; just follow your instinct.

Define Your Teaching North Star

Taking time to define what we know in our hearts and experience to be true about what students need and what teachers should provide is a powerful exercise. Our "truths" act as a North Star to guide us on our way when things seem overly complicated and we are overwhelmed.

I invite you to define your truths for yourself, and use them as a compass to help you navigate the challenges ahead in teaching.

Don't cheat yourself out of this exercise if you are new to teaching and think you don't have enough experience to define this yet.
Let your instinct guide you.

Here are my "truths" about what students need to feel in order to learn:

1. _____
2. _____
3. _____
4. _____

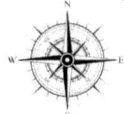

© Grace Stevens 2023

Define Your Teaching North Star

Here are my "truths" about teaching:

1. _____

2. _____

3. _____

4. _____

Reflection
How can I use these "truths" to form a compass to guide me when I am pulled in too many directions?

© Grace Stevens 2023

The Revolutionary Behind the Door

THERE ARE SHOCKINGLY FEW NEW IDEAS IN EDUCATION. YET, IN twenty years of back-to-school professional development, I can't think of one where I wasn't presented with a new program, procedures, or curriculum. Some years, it was all three. But in truth, many of those new programs are old ideas that have been recycled, rebranded (new acronyms to learn and new posters to hang up), and designed to make a publisher or consulting group more money.

That may sound jaded, but it's accurate. It's like there's a massive pendulum swinging from one side to another. First, we're all focused on teaching students to learn through the whole language approach. Wait, new research says direct phonics instructions are more effective. Here's the new curriculum. Several years later, the pendulum is swinging back the other way, and now we're using core, authentic texts instead of awkward stories created around repeated phonics sounds. We're scrambling for storage space in cupboards for the old curriculum, and shaking our heads at how much just got spent on the new resources.

When I was a student teacher, my second-grade mentor teacher used thematic unit kits that she checked out from the district office. Her favorite was the oceans kit. It included math lessons on measuring and estimating shells, reading and writing assignments about tides, and ocean-focused science experiments. Every year she would dig out her "ocean box" and set up her sand table with natural shells, sand dollars, and starfish. Many students in our school had never seen the ocean or been to the beach, and using realia was especially important for our English language learners. Our district had over 50 unique thematic kits available ranging from ant habitats, bubbles, and secret spy writing with lemon juice. The students loved them, and they were so fun to teach.

Then came a massive push in education to use only a validated, scripted curriculum. You know, learning objectives on the board, everyone in the same grade needed to be on the same page in the scope and sequence. It's Tuesday, so we must all be teaching Unit two, Week 2, Day 2. Pack up that realia table, and bye-bye to the thematic units.

Fast-forward ten years, and then came the Next Generation Science Standards. Cue the mandatory professional development on "cross-curricular connections—CCCs." Yep. Precisely what we used to call "thematic units." Let's hope the County of Education Science Department held on to all those kits!

So, having sat through more than two decades worth of back-to-school professional development and new initiatives, I adopt the mindset of "Take what you need and leave the rest." I always suspect the excitement around the new programs will fizzle out after a few months or weeks. All those data sheets and rubrics your administrator requests to fill out weekly or quarterly will die a lonely death in their inbox. Stressing ourselves out over completing them leads to frustration and is such a waste of energy. New curriculum packages come with more "additional resources" than we could ever fit into our instruction. Years later, some of the additional resource packs are still in their original shrink-wrap, buried in our cupboards right alongside incomplete sets of math manipulatives. You know I'm right.

WHAT IS MY POINT HERE? I'M NOT TRYING TO BE PESSIMISTIC, JUST realistic.

On any given day, more will be required of us than we can ever complete.

Every year, there will be a new curriculum, new technology, and the latest and greatest instructional practices. Many will be abandoned or at least put on the back burner by winter break. We need to make peace with this.

We should remain open-minded about new initiatives and be willing to try new things. But at the same time, having a defined North Star can help us prioritize what we take on and what we intentionally let go. Knowing our North Star can clarify when we feel overwhelmed with all the things being thrown at us. It can keep us moving in the right direction when many outside distractions seem urgent but are not mission-critical.

THIS BOOK WILL PROVIDE YOU WITH MANY TOOLS AND SUGGESTIONS on how to do this, especially in the chapters on boundaries and balance. But for now, I will leave you with the single most beneficial piece of advice that I received from my teacher credentialing program.

> When I'm in the meetings I smile real nice and say "Yes, sir!" "Yes, sir!" but then when I close my classroom door I am a revolutionary." -
>
> -Dr. Kweku Smith

DR. SMITH TAUGHT THE FIRST CLASS ON THE FIRST DAY OF MY teacher credentialing program. That quote was probably the most important thing I learned. More than two decades later, I still find it empowering.

I am not advocating being deceitful or subversive. I am simply pointing out that we are professionals. We live and breathe in the classroom every day. People with varying agendas (many seeking to sell curriculum, programs, or services) will have opinions on what is currently working in education. Many of these people or organizations have not been in a classroom for years, if ever. As professionals, it is our responsibility to be open to new things. But at a certain point, we need to close the door to our classroom, follow our North Star, and do what we know is best for students. We weren't trained and hired simply to teach the curriculum. Our job is to teach children.

Summary

In an educational environment where things constantly change, so much external static competes for our attention and pulls our focus away from our students and what they truly need from us. Defining our North Star and who we want to be as teachers helps us prioritize tasks and feel empowered to let some tasks go. Defining our North Star can also help us clarify our values and guide us when we are overwhelmed or feeling lost.

Get Empowered:

Ways To Practice This Mindset Habit Starting Today

1 Complete the North Star exercise in the Workbook. To do this, ask yourself these fundamental questions:

- What do I know my students need from me to feel seen, safe, and supported in their learning?

- What are my fundamental values about teaching?

- Come up with no more than about 5-6 ideas. The bullet point format is fine.

- Remember that this exercise is for you. It's designed to help guide you when you feel overwhelmed or lost.

. . .

2 KEEP THINGS SIMPLE. When your to-do list seems overwhelming, ask yourself, "Who do I want to be today?" Ultimately, deciding how you will show up for students will make more impact than the number of tasks you complete.

3 TAKE WHAT YOU NEED, AND LEAVE THE REST.

Next time you attend a professional development meeting, adopt this mindset, "I am going to look for three practical ideas that will positively impact my students, and I will find them."

• Write the ideas or strategies on a sticky note.

• Instead of being frustrated about how much time is wasted and how much of the information could have been condensed, set your radar to find the three precious gems you can use.

• File the stack of papers or binder that was handed to you.

• Put the sticky note in your lesson plan book as a reminder of those three things.

• Try to implement them immediately before you forget.

• If you find you need more detail, you can always dust off that binder.

4

Separate Your Worth from Your Work

> I have spent my entire life either at the schoolhouse, on the way to the schoolhouse, or talking about what happens in the schoolhouse. Both my parents were educators, my maternal grandparents were educators, and for the past 40 years, I've done the same thing."

Rita Pierson's TED Talk 2013, *Every Kid Needs a Champion*

YOU HAVE NO DOUBT SEEN RITA PIERSON'S BEAUTIFUL TED TALK at least once. It profoundly affected me when I first saw it in 2013. In fact, her talk inspired the journal prompt, "Who can I champion this week?" in my *Positive Mindset Journal for Teachers*.

No one can question Rita's passion and wisdom. But learning that she died only a month after giving her famous talk made me reflect. The students she influenced in her 40 years of teaching and the reach of that talk, which has been viewed more than 15 million times, is a fantastic legacy. But is making teaching your entire life a good idea?

I LOVE TEACHING. AS A CHILD, I WOULD LINE UP MY DOLLS AND TEDDY bears, and, when he could be coaxed, my cat Tigger onto the landing of the stairs, and I would play teacher. I would assign homework, complete the homework, grade the homework...all the things.

My career took a long detour into the corporate world, but when, in my late thirties, I finally had my very own classroom, it truly felt like home. Nothing made me happier than setting up my room, choosing all the books, and labeling all the supplies. And then, when the students showed up, it was magical! I spent many happy days, hours, weeks, and years in that classroom with my students. When I say I loved teaching, I mean it. I felt it was everything I was supposed to be doing with my life.

Teaching was a wonderful part of my life, but I told myself it wasn't my whole life. I had children to raise, a house and garden to keep up, aging parents to care for, pets, many friends and hobbies, and, for the last twelve years of my career, a side hustle that I poured my heart and soul into.

I told myself repeatedly that teaching wasn't my whole life. I coached teachers on school/life balance, I wrote books about it, talked about it on podcasts.

DO YOU KNOW WHAT TEACHING WAS, THOUGH? IT WAS A MASSIVE part of my identity.

When I retired and the time came to pack up and give away twenty years of my school stuff, I was surprised by just how much of my life and, to be honest, my children's things had ended up in that classroom: books, games, puzzles, and work samples.

I tried not to add up the value of the 500+ beautiful books I gave away, the classroom decorations, the furniture, and the mountains of extra supplies I'd accumulated. It wasn't the financial value that was hard to reconcile but the emotional value.

Later that year, when it was time to downsize my house and move, I decided it was best to donate all of my school spirit t-shirts. By the time I took out shirts with school logos on and shirts that I had bought just for seasonal holidays or spirit week (rainbow theme, spread kindness like confetti, red for drug-free week, you know the drill) and shirts I'd bought to match my grade span teammates, I was left with just six shirts: four plain black, two plain white. It was the same with the sweatshirts. And let's not even talk about my coffee mug collection.

R<small>ITA</small> P<small>IERSON'S</small> <small>INTRODUCTION TO THAT FAMOUS</small> TED T<small>ALK</small> always gets laughs from the audience because we can completely relate to it: We're either at school, thinking about school, talking about school, or worrying about school, and so much of our identity is wrapped in this idea of being a teacher.

Our identity as teachers dominates our wardrobes and all of our teacher-themed possessions. Being a teacher dominates our friendships, and, for many, it dominates our social media habits. Think of the top ten accounts you follow on social media—chances are more than half of them are either fellow teachers or about teaching. Bored Teachers Comedy, anyone? It's all part of a phenomenon I call "#teacherlife." So much of our identity is wrapped up in what we do.

The Empowered Teacher Toolkit

. . .

MY ARGUMENT IN THIS CHAPTER IS THAT THIS PHENOMENON OF #teacherlife, whereby we connect so much of our identity and worth with our chosen work, is unhealthy for numerous reasons.

First and foremost, it does not allow for a balanced life, which can result in burnout.

In *Positive Mindset Habits for Teachers*, I wrote,

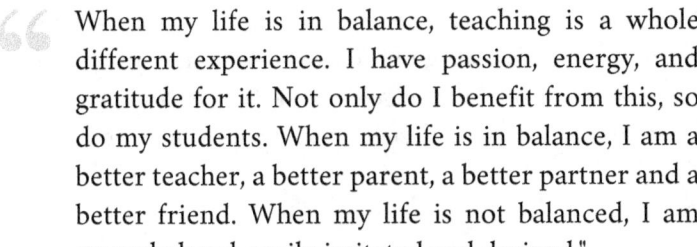

> When my life is in balance, teaching is a whole different experience. I have passion, energy, and gratitude for it. Not only do I benefit from this, so do my students. When my life is in balance, I am a better teacher, a better parent, a better partner and a better friend. When my life is not balanced, I am overwhelmed, easily irritated and drained."

WE HAVE MANY ROLES IN LIFE BEYOND BEING TEACHERS: WE'RE children, siblings, friends, maybe parents, partners, or coaches. These roles should all get equal airtime. We should also have interests and hobbies outside of teaching and working with students.

I was recently coaching a teacher and helping her find more balance in her life. From the outside, she appeared to have a full and rich life. She was always busy. In her spare time, she helped put on school plays, coached volleyball, led a youth group at church, and was very involved in her son's Boy Scout troop. When I asked her what she liked to do just for her that didn't involve being on a school campus or with students, she just looked at me blankly and said, "I honestly don't remember."

This teacher's situation is shockingly familiar. Many of us are in a season of life where most of our duties will involve either our children or, as a teacher, other people's children. But we should never lose sight of the fact that we all have an identity and an intrinsic worth beyond our role as carers of children.

A large portion of this book is dedicated to this topic. First, we will look at how to be intentional about how much school work you take on so that there is time left in the week for other roles and pleasures you have. Then, we will use a tool to diagnose where we're out of balance quickly to make a timely action plan before things get out of control. So, all that is coming, but for now, let's get back to why #teachingismywholelife is problematic.

BEYOND OUR LIFE BEING OUT OF BALANCE, THE OTHER ISSUE WHEN we attach our worth to our work is that we set ourselves up to fail. We will never feel that what we are doing is enough.

One of the frustrating parts of teaching is that we give so much of ourselves every day, work so hard, and care so much, and yet, most days, we don't get to see measurable and tangible results of all that effort and caring. It's not like we're in a trade where we have the satisfaction of seeing something we fixed, built, or created. We know that our work has an impact, and that's why we do it. But what evidence do we have of our impact?

SOME WILL ARGUE THAT WE HAVE TEST SCORES THAT CAN MEASURE our results. But we all know that a student's worth and growth cannot be reduced to mere data points on a graph. In the same way, we can't measure a teacher's effectiveness by those data meetings. Even with positive academic growth data, we are often unaware if or how we have genuinely impacted a student's life from a self-esteem, confidence, and social/emotional growth standpoint.

If we teach elementary-grade children, it's lovely to be validated by all the cute drawings and "You're my favorite teacher!" love notes. Middle and upper-grade teachers are more likely to have students come back to them, maybe years after the fact, and let them know what a profoundly positive impact they had on their lives. Those moments of validation are unforgettable and what we dreamed of when we labored hard to obtain our credentials.

But these moments are the exception, not the average day in the classroom. Many days are challenging, stressful, and tedious. Few teachers are idolized like we see in the movies. Even Mr. Holland had to put in thirty relatively thankless years of grinding and struggling against the backdrop of music funding budget cuts before he received his famous opus.

THAT MIGHT SOUND A LITTLE HARSH FOR A BOOK ABOUT empowering mindsets. But it's important to be realistic. There is a danger in equating so much of our identity and worth to how well things are going with our students. We have very few tangible measures of our impact, and many student success factors are beyond our control. If we don't have a strong sense of who we are and our intrinsic value to the world, inside and outside of the classroom, then we will be in for a bumpy and overwhelming ride.

Our teacher hearts all know the magic of hearing a student who was previously struggling with a concept say, "Oh, now I get it!"

We revel in the quiet satisfaction of observing students collaborating and working together to ensure their classmates' success. That's the fuel that keeps us going. But it doesn't necessarily translate to numbers on a page, upward motion on a growth chart, and the prerequisite percentage of data points in the "proficient" and "above proficient" columns of our school site growth plan.

So, when we don't separate our worth from our work, our lives will be out of balance, and we're setting ourselves up to fail. Our results will never be good enough. If we meet all the critical benchmarks for success in one year, the bar will be set higher the following year.

Let's be honest. In most schools, administrators are just as overwhelmed as teachers. They want to make their lives easier. So if a teacher is highly capable of remediating academic deficiencies, has good classroom management skills (meaning they don't send students to the office), works well with parents (meaning parents never call the office), and generally gets on with things without complaint they are an administrator's dream employee. Instead of being rewarded, that dream teacher will find a disproportionate number of students with challenging behaviors, academic gaps, or high-maintenance parents on their roster. If they are crushing it with test score growth one year, they are given even more academically struggling students the following year. It's not by evil design; it's simply due to convenience.

Another problem with equating our worth with our work is that we are setting ourselves up for potential heartache.

Many of us are conditioned to see teaching not just as a job but as a vocation, a calling, if you will. Like nursing or being a first responder, teaching is undoubtedly something you need to have a passion for. It's just too difficult, otherwise. But teaching is a job. Despite the "we are family here" messaging that many school cultures promote, it's an occupation, not an adoption. Anyone who has agonized, lost sleep, and cried for weeks before painfully submitting their resignation, only to see their job posted for a replacement before the day ends, can attest to having learned that lesson the hard way. This is even more true for anyone unexpectedly let go from a teaching or administrator position. As the saying goes, *"Lots of people are convenient. No one is indispensable."*

LAST BUT NOT LEAST, CONSIDER THIS. THE DAY WILL COME WHEN you will no longer be a teacher. You may have a long and rewarding career and, even after retirement, find a way to volunteer at a school or fill in as a substitute teacher because it brings you joy. But still, the fact remains that you won't be a teacher forever.

If teaching has been your whole identity and how you equate your value in the world, who will you be without teaching? In the same way that some parents struggle with an empty nest when their children go off into the world independently, you may face an identity crisis and a struggle to see how you fit into the world and contribute to it.

Even with all I know and all I teach, I still struggle with this. My vision for my life was always to learn and to teach. I am still an avid learner. And I still teach, but in a different way. I spend much time coaching educators, writing about teaching (blogs, books, emails), and talking about teaching (so many podcast episodes). Still, I get pangs when I see back-to-school supplies, kids on their way to school, and charming classroom set-ups on social media. I miss teaching and being with students in a way that people who aren't teachers don't understand. But I know I have intrinsic value to this world even if I never teach anybody anything again. Because of who I am, what I think, and how I love, not because of what I do.

And the same is true of you, too.

Summary

Teaching is a verb; it's not an identity. It's what we do; it's not who we are.

Equating our worth to our work not only leads to a life out of balance but also sets us up to feel constantly inadequate, as so many aspects of student outcomes are beyond our control. It can also lead to an identity crisis when we finally leave the profession. We must recognize that our worth in this world is intrinsic and independent of our contributions to education.

Get Empowered!

Ways To Practice This Mindset Habit Starting Today

1 Take time to become aware of your roles beyond that of a teacher. The exercise in the Companion Workbook can help you do this.

First, list all your roles in life. For me, those would include a teacher, friend, daughter, sister, mother, partner, coach, podcaster, and writer.

Then, list interests and passions that are just for you and not necessarily related to your roles. For example, for me, they would include reading, quilting, salsa dancing, pickleball, yoga, cooking, and gardening.

Then, reflect on how much time you give those other passions. For example, for years, I would list yoga as a hobby. But if I were honest with myself, my yoga mat had sat collecting dust in the corner for so long that it would have cracked if I tried to roll it out. I wanted to think it was a hobby. But for it to be considered an active hobby, I would need to engage in it, not just buy the equipment and pay for the membership I don't use.

Separate Your Identity (who you are) from What You Do

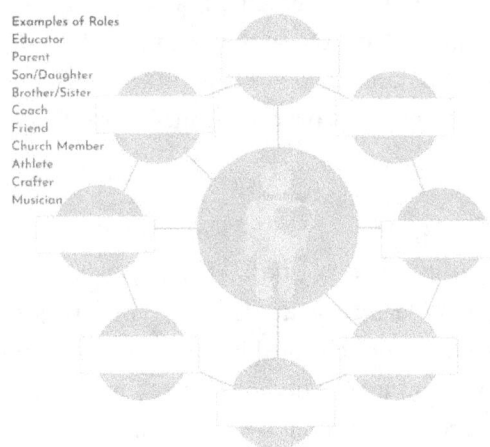

Examples of Roles
Educator
Parent
Son/Daughter
Brother/Sister
Coach
Friend
Church Member
Athlete
Crafter
Musician

© Grace Stevens 2023

2. Don't be discouraged if the exercise makes you realize that it's been a while since you've engaged in any activities just for you. Sometimes, this is just a function of our season of life.

When I was full-time teaching, raising my children, and building a business, I would be proud of myself if I could still get on a long bike ride with my friends on the weekend. That would fill two buckets - exercise and social interaction. But if you realize that it's been a while since you even thought about indulging in a non-child-related passion, set aside some quiet time to reflect - what did you love to do before you became a teacher? What do you find yourself drawn to that you see other people doing? A large part of being an effective teacher is being a lifelong learner. What have you always wanted to try? An instrument? A recreational sport? A new craft? Binge-watching true crime doesn't count. You want to think about fun hobbies or activities that have tangible results. For me, that's one reason I love quilting. I get to hang out with my quilting friends, and I can produce something tangible that I can gift to people. I also find it very satisfying to see the progress I've made over the years as I've honed my craft.

3. Consider conducting a quick time audit of your day. See if there are any times in your day that you are just passively consuming media or not engaged in mission-critical things. Even scheduling 15-20 minutes daily for yourself and your interests is enough to ensure that teaching isn't your entire life. If you have a family to look after, you may only be able to carve out 20 minutes for yourself by getting up earlier before your family members get up and make demands of you. While getting up even earlier is not likely appealing, developing a habit of having

your own time every day, just for a while, is very important for your mental health.

My best advice is to put yourself and that time on the calendar and treat it as non-negotiable, just like any other appointment. If you wait to find time on your calendar for yourself, you won't. You need to be intentional about scheduling time for your new interest and following through just as you would if it were an appointment with a parent, a doctor, or a dentist. We need to be as diligent about keeping our commitments to ourselves as we are about keeping our commitments to others.

4. PAY EXTRA ATTENTION TO THE CHAPTER IN THIS BOOK ABOUT busting the school-life balance myth. The Wheel of School and Life Balance exercise will diagnose the areas of your life that are significantly out of balance. Equating our worth to our work is part of the same issue—everything is always about school. In order to have balance and feel fulfilled, we need less school and more life.

5

Focus on What You Can Control

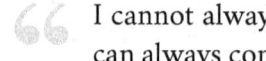 I cannot always control what goes on outside. But I can always control what goes on inside."

– Wayne Dyer Author & Spiritual Teacher

The Accidental Path

If you had told me thirty years ago that I'd end up coaching teachers on having a more positive life experience, I would have rolled my eyes so hard it would have risked permanent injury. Or that I would eventually get certified in Neuro-Linguistic Programming and Life Coaching (with an emphasis on "Emotional Intelligence," no less) … seriously, I would have laughed and called you crazy. Nothing could have been further from my radar.

Yet here we are.

. . .

I REMEMBER THE FIRST TIME I WAS EXPOSED TO ANY SORT OF "personal development" ideas. Trust me, I did not go seeking them out. I was reluctant, skeptical, and very uncomfortable when they were thrust upon me.

Here's the story.

I worked in the corporate world and had been promoted to a branch manager role. I was sent away for a week for management and sales training. It was in a fancy hotel with a generous expense account. Everyone was wearing their best 90s power suits, sensible briefcases in hand.

Truthfully, I was a little insecure about that briefcase. I was worried that my peers might realize it was not an original Coach briefcase but a cheap knockoff I had purchased from Ross Dress for Less. I felt the real item would convey to the world that I "had arrived." From where, I wasn't sure. But I was young and excited to prove myself and was still a long way from learning that happiness and validation have little to do with acquiring "things" or the trappings of traditional status symbols. I was barely twenty-five years old.

Anyway, I found myself in a room full of twenty or so strangers, all eager to learn how to elicit maximum productivity from our staff (no one was calling them "teams" back then) and close the most sales with the highest gross margin. It was all about the money and the awards. Let's do this!

So, imagine my surprise when the first presenter handed everyone a worksheet with two concentric circles on it and asked us to write "everything we were worried about" in the larger, outer circle. What the actual heck?

. . .

Maybe you don't know this about me, but I grew up in London. I ended up living in California somewhat accidentally, and at twenty-five and pretty recently transplanted, I was still feeling very much like an outsider from a cultural standpoint.

I was raised in a traditional British "stiff upper lip" and "we don't discuss our emotions" environment. My family's primary survival mechanism was to pretend bad things never happened and, if they did, never to discuss them. Therapy was seen as something only weak, self-indulgent people participated in. The idea that anyone would articulate they craved a more positive life experience or for things to be somehow different than they were was "shameful," "ungrateful," and quite frankly, "very American." We simply "got on with things" without complaining. Yikes.

Of course, I'm not advocating any of that. It took me years and considerable effort to reverse that completely unproductive mindset.

But at that time, I was concerned that my company was investing a lot of money in order for me to learn how to blow my sales quota out of the water, so why were we wasting time talking about our worries and our feelings?

I was very uncomfortable. It suddenly seemed that being judged for my fake Coach briefcase was the least of my worries.

It occurred to me that maybe the exercise was some sort of test or trap. For example, when an interviewer asks you, "What are your weaknesses?" It should be evident that the correct answer is not to expose a true weakness but to respond with something appealing to a hiring manager. So, "I waste a lot of time on social media" is an inappropriate answer, but "I'm a workaholic" is a winner.

I hurriedly scribbled that one of my concerns was "Not meeting my branch's sales goals" in the outer circle. That seemed vulnerable enough but work-related and also demonstrated my drive to succeed. When we were called on to "share out" (good grief, could this get any worse?), a huge young man from Texas volunteered he was worried about this: his wife was not watering their newly planted sod and that when he got home after a week, his lawn would be dead.

It's been over 30 years, but I still remember that so clearly. A grown man at a sales meeting where no one knew him, where he "should" be making a power play to impress, saying he was worried about his lawn.

Another woman shared she had just lost 30 pounds (due to a divorce, no less!) and was worried that she would put some of it back on during the week while eating hotel food and not preparing meals for herself.

I was panic-stricken. Who were these people, and why were they oversharing? And how was I ever going to get through this week?

We were presented with Stephen Covey's *The Seven Habits of Highly Effective People*. The exercise with the circles was one of the first exercises in the book.

ON THE SURFACE, THIS EXERCISE WAS ABOUT CIRCLES OF Influence versus Circles of Control. I have since used this exercise hundreds of times with my staff in the corporate world, with students in my classroom, and when coaching teachers. It's a simple exercise that helps solidify the mindset we will explore in this chapter. But on a deeper level, this experience was so much more. It introduced to me the following concepts:

- The idea of being proactive versus reactive (that we can **choose** how to respond to situations)
- The idea of taking **personal responsibility** for what we are creating in our life
- The idea that our **choices** determine our outcomes, not just our circumstances
- The idea of paradigm shifts and that **things are not simple as they are but as we perceive them to be**
- The concept of embracing a mindset of **collaboration** will reap better results than one of competition
- And ultimately, it gave me the language to express how I wanted to live my life - **Principle Centered.**

DR. COVEY'S BOOK BLEW MY MIND. IT SHOOK ME OUT OF AN unconscious victim mentality and set me on a personal growth path I am still on today.

I cannot overstate this. I was at once overjoyed with the feeling of empowerment that Dr. Covey's ideas presented but also frustrated. I considered myself well-educated. Despite my humble beginnings, I was pretty "book smart" and was fortunate enough to have teachers who pushed me and helped me get scholarship grants. Consequently, I attended university in four different countries and different cultures. How on earth had I never been exposed to these ideas before?

It was as if Dr. Covey's now classic book had hit me in the head upside the head and said,

- Understand your part in creating your experience
- You can be a better version of yourself today than you were yesterday

- Your only competition is yourself
- The only person that gets in your way is you
- Your experience of your life is based on the quality of your thoughts
- And ultimately (not in this book, but in the dozens and dozens of books I felt inspired to read after), **you don't need to believe every stupid thought you think.**

You get the picture. The idea that I could control my mindset, which in turn controlled my feelings and actions, was empowering, exciting, and liberating. Maybe it sounds overly simplistic, but once Dr. Covey planted the idea in my head that I had control of my life, I was off and running. Meeting sales quotas no longer seemed like a daunting challenge.

Over the thirty-plus years since that experience, I have read books, participated in seminars, bought classes, courses, and coaching, invested in some pretty nerdy certifications, read a ridiculous amount of research about how the brain works, and vowed to share these ideas, when and where appropriate, with my classroom and students. But truthfully, everything I discovered in all that time since has been some variation of the critical learning I summarized above from that precious, dog-eared, and often reread book.

Applying This in the Classroom

A quick aside: Someone reading this book will undoubtedly feel compelled to put me on blast and point out that Dr. Covey is a devout Mormon. While some feel his work has religious undertones, I found all of the ideas in his book to be secular and ultimately promote **personal empowerment**.

I am religiously unaffiliated and passionately believe that there should be no "religious" agenda in public schools. But let me just reassure you that any educator can benefit from my work. I have no hidden agenda or bias other than to give teachers the tools necessary for a more positive teaching experience.

I teach based on brain science, psychology, and behavioral therapy. Can it seem a little "new agey" to some? Sure. But it's helpful to adopt the mindset I adopted for every teacher professional development session over the last twenty years - take what resonates and leave the rest. You don't need to be "wowed" by every strategy or mindset to find transformative value in this book.

BACK TO THE CRITICAL POINT: *IF WE WANT TO HAVE A MORE POSITIVE, peaceful, and proactive experience in our classrooms, we need to learn to differentiate the things we control from the things we don't and focus our emotional energy on only the former.*

Let me give you some quick examples.

What we don't have control over is the weather. We have control over proactively setting up a plan for the dreaded rainy day recess.

We don't have control over our school district's or state's policy in administering standardized tests. We have control over how we present this challenge to our students, how much time we spend preparing them, and how much mental energy we spend worrying about the results.

And one more example because it is still so divisive. We can't control how many students and families have been fully vaccinated for Covid or other infectious diseases. What we can control is the procedures that we set up in our classroom to keep everyone as safe as possible. This can include promoting a culture of non-judgment of students who still elect to wear masks when colds and flu are in season because that is what makes them most comfortable or what their parents want them to do.

You are getting the general idea here. Investing our time and energy in things we can influence will be more resourceful and helpful and, ultimately, make us feel better than wasting energy worrying, talking about, or complaining about things over which we have no control.

Completing the Exercise - Concerns v. Control

Let's look at the exercise. There is a blank sample in the Companion Workbook that you can print out. But first, let's look at the concept. You can also do this with students by drawing two concentric circles on a page if you don't want to be fancy.

Apply The Strategy

Circle of

Circle of Influence

Concern

Things I'm Worried About → *Where do they belong?* → Things I Have Control Over

List them here

List them here

© Grace Stevens Happy-Classrooms.com · Adapted from Stephen Covey's Work · 7 Habits of Highly Effective People

IN THE OUTER CIRCLE, JOT DOWN ALL OF THE THINGS THAT YOU ARE concerned about. These can be issues in your classroom, on your campus, or with education in general. Of course, we are more than just teachers. We have human needs and concerns, such as physical, mental, emotional, spiritual, and financial health. We also have family and people we love. So that's a whole lot of potential concerns. But for this exercise, let's keep it school-focused.

In the inner circle, write which of those concerns you have any degree of control over.

Note: try to complete the exercise before you look at this list so you are not influenced by it.

BE AWARE THAT FOR MOST PEOPLE, IT'S A LOT EASIER TO THINK OF things we worry about. Don't beat yourself up about this. It doesn't mean that you are a "negative" person or that you are stuck. It's a very normal response hard-wired into our biology. Worry about things keeps us safe. Here are some examples of items that might be in your circles:

CIRCLE OF CONCERN

The number of students on your roster

How your students show up (especially those from at-risk or unstable backgrounds or students with trauma and behavior issues)

The parents of the students on your roster

The people in your grade level/departmental teammates

Your administrator, Superintendent, and local school board

The physical condition of your campus and its resources

The classroom you are assigned

The grade level you are assigned

The curriculum you are required to teach

Your salary schedule

Standardized tests you are required to administer

School/district rules, policies and procedures

Students who don't care about doing their work or the quality of it

What other people think of you

What other teachers are doing in their room, or how they handle discipline

Circle of Influence/Control

Your attitude

How you prioritize your mental, physical, and emotional health

Your thoughts and actions

The goals you set

How you handle challenges

How you set boundaries with people (more on this later)

How much time and energy you invest in building classroom community

How creatively you teach the curriculum

How proactive you are in seeking out opportunities for support or professional development in areas that you may be struggling (for example, classroom management or dealing with difficult parents)

How involved you get with school leadership committees, your local union (if you have one), parent clubs, and school board meetings to work towards positive change

Creating lessons that are as engaging as possible

Arranging and managing supports and interventions for students who need extra help

Consider that the entire circle area (inner and outer rings) represents your total time and energy in a day or any given moment. Time and emotional energy are finite resources. The more you focus on the area of control, the more it expands and the smaller the circle of concern gets. In the same way, the more time and energy you spend focusing on things in your outer circle of concern, the smaller your circle of influence becomes.

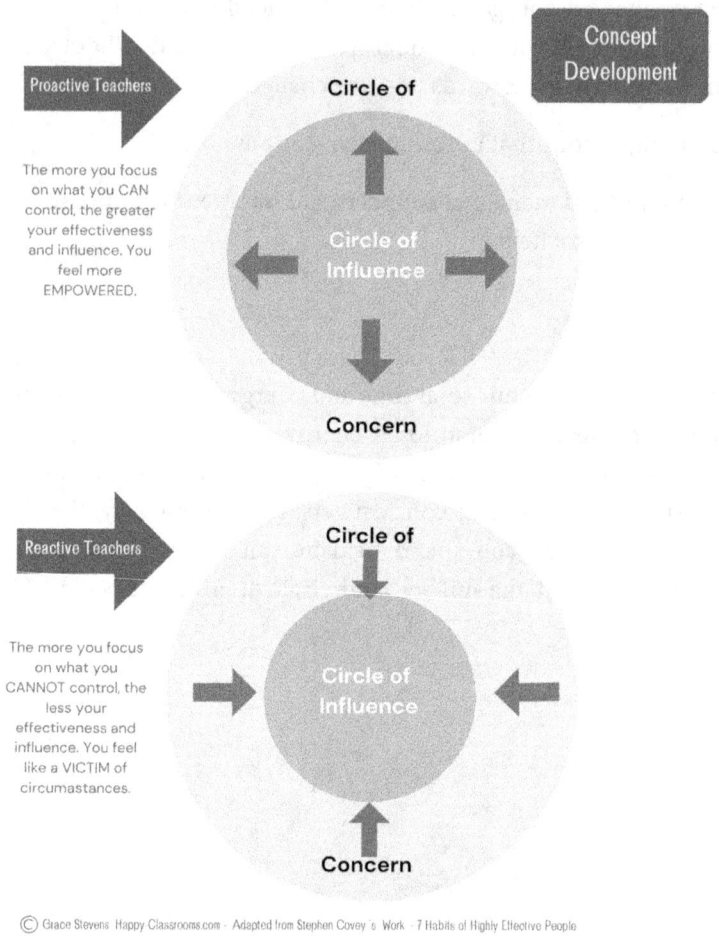

OVER-INVESTING TIME AND ENERGY IN OUR CIRCLE OF CONCERNS leads to the following:

- Frustration
- Overwhelm

- Feelings of hopelessness
- Feelings of helplessness
- Anxiety
- Depression
- Feeling victimized

Consciously investing in our circle of control leads to the following:

A sense of empowerment

We don't need a list of benefits. A sense of empowerment is plenty. It's the opposite of living in a "victim" mentality where we feel we are at the whim of external circumstances over which we have no control. A sense of empowerment reduces stress, overwhelm, anxiety, apathy, and depression. It wards off burnout and is at the heart of job satisfaction.

Proactive versus Reactive

Feeling empowered and taking more responsibility for the results in our lives fall under the broader topic of being proactive rather than reactive. But for now, let's define what being proactive means at its core.

Being proactive means recognizing that you have choices in creating and influencing situations and outcomes rather than just responding to situations after the fact. It means that you prepare yourself and take positive actions before a situation happens. You search for solutions rather than just focusing on identifying and lamenting problems. Proactive people focus on what they can control.

Dr. Covey summarizes it perfectly:

> Proactive people focus their efforts in the Circle of Influence. They work on the things they can do something about. The nature of their energy is positive, enlarging and magnifying, causing their Circle of Influence to increase. Reactive people, on the other hand, focus their efforts in the Circle of Concern...The negative energy generated by that focus, combined with neglect in areas they could do something about, causes their Circle of Influence to shrink."

FOR ME, BECOMING MORE PROACTIVE CAME WITH AGE AND experience. As I repeatedly experienced certain uncomfortable situations, I asked myself, "Where is my responsibility for what is happening right now?" I learned to explore what my perceptions were, what I was thinking, what I said, and how I acted. I realized that I always had a choice in how I reacted to things. Many ways that I reacted were simply a result of habit and conditioning. A shift in perception was necessary.

Few of us learned these skills in school unless we recently graduated. The good news is that the focus on "Growth Mindset" in recent years is starting to challenge students to think this way. We can choose what we think, which influences how we feel, and make new neural pathways that move beyond habit and social conditioning. We can better influence our outcomes when we change how we think, feel, act, or react.

. . .

Consider the traditional ways to compare proactive versus reactive language.

Reactive Language	Proactive Language
There's nothing I can do	How can I positively influence this situation?
I can't help feeling this way	I have the ability to choose my response
This always happens!	What can I do to change this outcome?
I can't do this	I can see this differently

Compare these with typical fixed mindset versus growth mindset language common in many classrooms today.

Fixed Mindset	Growth Mindset
I'm no good at this	I'm still learning how to do this
I messed up	Mistakes help me learn
I give up	I'll try a different way
Messing up makes me a failure	I only fail if I give up

As you can see, the foundational premise in both models is the same. It has been so exciting to see these ideas normalized in teaching, and we all owe a great debt to Dr. Carol Dweck's research and her excellent book *Mindset: The New Psychology of Success.*

Just as intelligence isn't fixed, neither is our ability to be proactive or reactive. **We can learn to be more proactive.** Learning to apply our focus on things that we can influence is the first step.

Dealing With Student Trauma

One of the areas that causes the most stress to teachers is an area that is rarely discussed in education. It's an area that falls under the banner of "setting boundaries," but I am including it in this chapter because it ultimately has to do with things beyond our control. It is the problem of absorbing and carrying around the trauma that students experience outside school. This phenomenon is often called "vicarious trauma" and even "second-hand PTSD." It's real, it's damaging, and it's something that we need to be proactive about minimizing.

FOR SIXTEEN YEARS, I TAUGHT AT A RURAL TITLE 1 SCHOOL. Ninety percent of the students qualified for free lunch, breakfast, busing, and after-school care. We had a dentist volunteer once a week, and we coordinated with a local church to distribute food packages on Friday nights so that students and their families had something to eat on the weekends.

Beyond poor economic circumstances, many of these students had unstable family backgrounds. One year, out of nine first-grade boys in my room, five had fathers in jail, and another had PTSD after his mother died of a drug overdose in her car on Christmas Eve. That's the kind of detail you just never forget. Another boy had experienced so much trauma in his foster care situation that he had residual physical and emotional deficits and needed a full-time aide because he was a constant flight risk. He was adept at escaping, and it wasn't a game to him; it was a survival instinct. His aide also had to cover the lunchroom, yard, and dismissal as part of her responsibilities, so when she finally took her breaks, it was up to me to chase around school after him. That same year, one of my female students was sexually assaulted in the school bathroom when she was participating in the after-school program. She was six.

It was a small school in an even smaller community. Many parents didn't speak English, and it was not unusual for school staff to help parents with paperwork and procuring services outside of the educational realm. I made countless calls to social workers during my time there, including the sheriff and Child Protective Services. When one of our beloved students shot himself in the head in a game of Russian Roulette (possibly a gang initiation), my colleague arranged the funeral for the parents and facilitated fundraising to pay for it. Many of us who had taught this student and his younger sister was in my class at the time of his tragic death. We were devastated and left with a huge sense of guilt - what had we missed? The person who had given him the gun had also been one of our students. He was 13 years old.

Compounding the stress was that we were a small school district with limited resources. We shared our one counselor and psychologist with four other districts. Most years, we didn't have a nurse. Teachers and administrators took on roles we had never imagined or been trained in. The emotional toll was exhausting and it was a constant struggle to remain optimistic.

I could continue, but these are all scenarios that are painfully familiar to many of you.

And yet, I loved my time at that school. The sense of community was amazing, and while the responsibilities were often overwhelming, the freedom to be creative and carve out truly magical teaching experiences was empowering. The payback was seeing a positive impact on many student lives.

. . .

For various reasons, I left that school district after 16 years. It wasn't necessarily due to all of the student trauma, but I naively thought one bonus of moving to a school in a higher socioeconomic environment would mean I would see a lot less of it. I was excited that I could finally "focus on actually teaching."

My new school environment could not have been more different. It was in a very affluent community, with involved, highly educated parents and absolutely no shortage of resources. So, did I get to devote all of my energy to providing a challenging curriculum and 21st-century skills? Nope. There was still plenty of student trauma to go around. Was the student who never took off his hoodie always cold or hiding the evidence of self-harm? More than one of my students experienced such extreme online bullying they stopped coming to school. A colleague from my original school also left to work in a larger, more affluent school district. In her first year, she lost one student to suicide, and another died of leukemia. Tragically, the only school counselor on their campus to support students and staff through these terrible situations also died from Covid.

I'm not telling you anything you don't already experience for yourself. There is no magic school where student trauma isn't a constant. Its economics may vary, but the effect is still the same. It is constant and there's no escaping it.

We spend up to 30 hours a week with our students. We get to know and care for them, and if we are great at what we do, we get to create a very special classroom community that feels like a family in many ways. For example, we may not enjoy them all the same (there's always that crazy uncle), but they all belong, and we have mutual responsibilities to ensure everyone is OK.

Constantly being exposed to our students' trauma increases teacher stress and leaves us prone to emotional and physical exhaustion. If we are not vigilant, we also risk becoming desensitized, numb, or indifferent. This is called "Compassion Fatigue" and is a phenomenon that affects many health care, social services, and emergency relief workers.

SO, HOW CAN WE SPEND OUR DAY WITH STUDENTS, ENCOURAGE AND support them, and help them grow while also being able to "turn it off" when we walk off campus?

How do we avoid the stress of internalizing student trauma and not worrying about our students when we are at home?

And how do we do this without hardening ourselves so that it no longer affects us and we lose our ability to truly empathize?

One solution is to regularly ask ourselves, "Is this something that is in my control or not?"

Let's think back to our two circles and consider some examples.

Things I am Concerned About	Things I Can Control
The student comes from a chaotic background	Providing a calm, safe, consistent classroom environment
The student coming to school hungry	Having snacks available in class
The student comes in with bruises	Sending the student to the nurse who can probe further and confidentially
The student seems really "out of sorts" for a prolonged period	See if the counselor can meet with the student. Most school policies allow students to talk to counselors once before they need their parents' permission.
You suspect a student's family has been sleeping in their car and is unhoused.	Refer the situation to the office and see if they can provide a "well check."

As you can see, many of these action items involve other agencies and professionals on campus or in your district. Our job is to teach. No matter how much we want to be, we can't be all things to all students.

Many schools are underfunded in these areas and do not have adequate support from these types of professionals. But constantly dwelling on that fact leads to frustration and hopelessness. If we want to feel empowered, we must focus on the areas we can control. One action item could be participating in school board meetings and advocating for more resources in these areas. Did we try once, and nothing happened? Possibly. But progress won't be made unless we keep trying.

I don't have a magic wand. It really boils down to being proactive about positively influencing the situation as much as possible and then learning to detach ourselves.

THIS I DO KNOW FOR SURE. INTERNALIZING STUDENT TRAUMA AND worrying about it when we are at home does nothing to help the student. It only serves to steal our time and presence from our family and contribute to our stress, sleeplessness, and burnout.

We are adults and professionals. It is our responsibility to protect our own mental space and our peace so that we can show up as our best selves and help all of us students, not just those experiencing trauma.

Proactively take action, feel content that you have positively influenced the areas of the student situation over which you have control, and then make peace with the fact that you need to let the rest go. In order to be productive and effective, we need to take not only a physical break from school at the end of the day but also a mental one.

Summary

If we want to have a more positive, peaceful, and proactive experience in our classrooms, we need to learn to differentiate the things we have control over from the things we don't and focus our emotional energy on only the former.

Investing our time and energy in things we can influence will be more resourceful and helpful and, ultimately, make us feel better than wasting energy worrying, talking about, or complaining about things over which we have no influence.

Get Empowered

Ways To Practice This Mindset Habit Starting Today

1 Complete the Circles of Influence/Circles of Control exercise in the Companion Workbook. Consider printing out extra copies of the worksheet and putting them in your planner to revisit quarterly or whenever you need to boost your sense of empowerment.

2 DEPENDING ON THEIR AGE, CONSIDER COMPLETING THE EXERCISE with students.

3 IDENTIFY ONE AREA AT SCHOOL OR IN YOUR CLASSROOM THAT takes up much of your time or your mental and emotional energy. Determine if any aspect of this problem could fall into your circle of control. Proactively think of two to three things you could do to improve this situation. If you can do nothing, is

there a mindset you could adopt or a different way to view the situation that might make it less stressful?

4 Educate yourself on resources available to help at-risk students. Again, you cannot be all things to all students.

5 Connect with your school/district counselor, psychologist, nurse, behavior interventionist, or any other professional who can support students with their social and emotional needs. Build relationships with them. Ask them to provide a list of resources and referrals to outside agencies.

6 If you want resources for your classroom and students, consider a low-time investment way of raising funds. One excellent resource that takes very little time is DonorChoose.org. Teachers can set up a free account and add projects they would like funded. Private individuals and corporations donate any amount until the project is funded.

I posted my first request for a project for my classroom over a decade ago, and I have never known a project not get funded. My requests ranged from class sets of books, headphones for students, and sensory wiggle seats to art supplies, science projects (live insects to hatch in my classroom—fun!), and technology.

Here are some best practices from my experience. First, it takes about 20 minutes to set up your account and class bio. But after that, setting up other projects is quick and easy. You can even attach an Amazon wishlist.

Next, start with a lower ticket request—$200 or below—so it will be quickly funded.

Once you get it funded, send thank you notes from your class and upload pictures of the resource being used. Photograph students from behind or just show their hands using the to avoid having to collect permission slips allowing the use of their image.

Finally, when you post the project request, share the link that DonorsChoose.org gives you with parents and others. Someone you know might work for a company that "matches" donations or has a special relationship with the organization. I once had a project 100 % funded in just a few hours because a large company had pledged a certain amount of money to fund any "technology" type request.

7   IF YOU'VE NEVER READ *THE 7 HABITS OF HIGHLY EFFECTIVE People*, I cannot recommend it enough. I believe it's one of the five most-read books in the world.

IF YOU TEACH HIGH SCHOOL, CONSIDER EXPOSING YOUR STUDENTS to *The 7 Habits of Highly Effective Teens* by Sean Covey (Stephen's son). It is easy to read, with plenty of graphics to keep them interested, and it coaches teens in areas such as avoiding peer pressure, being a better friend, getting along with their parents, taking responsibility, and having a positive self-image. It has exercises and relatable stories about teens from all around the world. Be cautious if you feel your school board or parents might be sensitive to you recommending a book written by someone other than the predominant faith system of your community. It feels terrible to consider this, and it falls under the banner of "censorship," but we live and teach in the real world. The last thing I wish to do is lead you down a path of more stress.

6

Redefine Balance

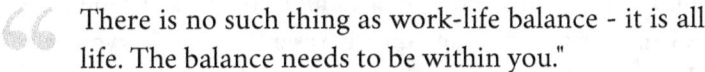 There is no such thing as work-life balance - it is all life. The balance needs to be within you."

- Sadhguru, Spiritual Thought Leader

ONE OF THE BENEFITS OF GROWING IN YEARS, EXPERIENCE, AND wisdom is that we get to change our minds without apologizing.

Six years ago, when I wrote *Positive Mindset Habits for Teachers*, I wrote a chapter called "Keep all of the Plates Spinning." It was a simpler, pre-pandemic time in education. I naively thought some magic formula or strategy existed for "getting it all done." Even back then, before all the crazy school life versus home life lines got blurred, any teacher would need more arms than an octopus to keep all the plates of their teacher responsibilities spinning in the air. And that's not even considering juggling any responsibilities they might have outside of school: kids, pets, aging parents, community responsibilities, and, for many of us, a second job or "side hustle."

So I'm calling bull crap on all of that. There is no magic strategy or tool to "get everything done."

I changed my mind.

In fairness, that had never been the point of the chapter. The point was about balance, prioritizing having a rich and full life outside of teaching, and "putting on your own oxygen mask first." Had I known we'd later spend over two years teaching through masks, I would have likely chosen a different metaphor. But that point remains valid: self-care first. We can't take care of the needs of others if we are exhausted, depleted, and "running on empty."

Again, I'll say, "Our energy teaches more than our lesson plans." Frazzled, overwhelmed, and quietly resentful that everyone else's needs come first is not a good classroom vibe. And it's no way to live outside the classroom, either.

ALL OF THE INFORMATION IN THIS BOOK IS GEARED TOWARDS getting you out of "survival mode" and moving past the mindset that meeting your needs can wait until the weekend, spring break, or summer, or when you have the "dream class," the perfect teaching partners, an actual prep period every day or when you retire.

News flash: Your life is happening now. Self-care, happiness, and being fiercely protective of your energy can not be put off until later or ignored. You need to be intentional and proactive about self-care. No one is coming to save you or to give you permission to "do less."

So, while we should not abandon the idea of striving for balance, a new, updated, and realistic approach is in order. We need a better metaphor.

Glass Versus Rubber Balls

Let's stick with the idea of juggling because even on the best of days, teaching is a bit of a circus. Let's say we're juggling balls, not spinning plates. The goal is to keep the most important balls in the air while intentionally choosing to drop less essential balls without experiencing guilt. Additionally, we need to realize that we have a choice about how many balls we juggle; we don't need to accept every new ball thrown at us lest we end up overwhelmed, ultimately dropping them all.

STEP ONE

So, step one is to make peace with the idea that we will never be able to do everything that is required of us. Getting it all done is not humanly possible. Even when we master setting boundaries, we will still have more things on our to-do list than we could ever comfortably accomplish.

If you've been teaching a while, you've likely discovered one of education's dirty secrets. That is that, if you appear to "have it all together" (as in you have not been caught either napping, crying, or hiding in your car or under your desk recently), then you will automatically be singled out to be "volunteered" for a new committee or extra responsibilities.

So, while we may aim to please and be considered "ultra-efficient" in our administrator's eyes, it is not wise to always be the first teacher to reply to emails, complete data tracking spreadsheets, etc. It unconsciously sends the message that we have time on our hands.

I hate to play games, but occasionally, it might be wise to strategically reply to an email from your admin or district office at 9 PM at night. I advocate not working at home, but sometimes, a passive-aggressive hint is in order. It can subtly remind our admin that we cannot achieve all of the "extra" things required during our contract hours.

Regardless of what you think of this idea, step one is still this: make peace with the idea that not everything we are required to do as teachers will get done.

As a former ultra-compliant, people-pleasing rule follower, I know this idea can be very uncomfortable. We fear judgment from other teachers, parents, and administrators. "What will people think?" can be a constant soundtrack playing in my head due to cultural and parental conditioning. But I'm here to tell you this: what evolved and intelligent people will think is this,

"Good for her, prioritizing herself, her family, her students, and her mental health over other people's agendas."

People may be judgmental and envious if they lack the skills and confidence to prioritize their responsibilities accordingly. It could also be because they are unhappy, judgmental, or just plain mean. Sadly, many overwhelmed people populate our faculty, campus, and parent bodies. In which case, should we even care what they think?

When I sensing people's judgment, I always remember Dr. Seuss' wise words:

Those who mind don't matter, and those who matter don't mind."

We need to change the narrative. An in-depth discussion on how to do so will follow in a separate chapter. But for now, just remember this tenant of my ECHO Framework for Educator Empowerment: other teachers' experience doesn't need to be your experience. Just because other teachers burn themselves out trying to "get it all done," it doesn't mean you need to.

Here's what I think: the world has enough martyrs. There is no prize for being the most stressed, exhausted, burned-out teacher on campus. We should be in awe of people who leave campus at a "decent" hour, not critical. The world needs energized, positive, and creative teachers who prioritize self-care so that teaching is sustainable.

So, let's recap. Step one: **Accept that there aren't enough hours in the day to get everything done. We have to be intentional about what we choose to do.**

STEP TWO:

Prioritize everything on our ridiculously long to-do list into two categories. One category is what we are calling "glass balls," and the other is "rubber balls."

I cannot take credit for this analogy. Brian Dyson, the former CEO of Coca-Cola, used it in his commencement speech at Georgia Tech University in 1991. Before this, I could not find evidence of the analogy, so I apologize if its origin predates that. Regardless, this concept can help us clarify which items on our to-do list we should intentionally "drop" or put off until another time.

So here is how this works. The idea is that glass balls are a top priority. They are the items that need to be completed for the week and the items that only you can do. These items will vary week by week. Sometimes, the glass balls will be work-related. At school, there are things on the school calendar that are "non-negotiable" as far as timing goes. They are things you would need help to pass off to a substitute teacher or delegate to student helpers. They are not things you can "drop" and pick up another time because they are made of glass and will shatter.

Here are some examples of school-related "glass balls":

- Report cards/end of the grading period

- Back to School Night/Open House

- Parent/teacher conference week

- Athletic tournaments that you coach

- Academic competitions that you coach or organize (Science Fair, Spelling Bee, Math Decathlon, etc.)

- Theater, choir, or orchestra performances you are involved in

- State Testing

- Off-site activities - science camp, field trips

- Graduation - both organizing the event (you unsung heroes!) and, for non-organizers, attending the event if it is mandated by your contract

- Committees that you signed up for or were assigned to you. For example, curriculum committee, safety committee, leadership committee, writing committee, student council ... the list of committees is endless.

- Anything that is dictated by your union or school "contract" that you signed

RUBBER BALLS ARE ITEMS ON YOUR LIST THAT DON'T "BREAK" IF YOU let them fall for a while. They will bounce, and you can pick them up another time. Or, let them roll away and wait to see if your administrator sends another email about them.

Intentionally ignoring requests and directives may sound unprofessional, but I am discussing the real world here. Almost every year, there is a new "focus," program, or acronym that someone who has little to do with your classroom has decided is a priority. New procedures, complete with tracking sheets, are given, and within weeks, there is no more follow-up. We're tracking data no one is checking because new priorities have emerged or our administrator realizes that the one-hour training we were forced to sit through at the beginning of the year in professional development was insufficient for us to implement the program correctly.

I know firsthand how frustrating this is. It helps to remember that our principals or head teachers were often not asked for their input on the programs, so they have as little "buy-in" as some teachers. So yes, you can test the waters with some "rubber balls" and see if they can roll away and be forgotten. Wait for that reminder email. If it was that mission-critical, you can chase after the ball and take care of it.

Here are some examples of school-related "rubber balls":

- Replying to every email (see above). If it's super important, somebody will send a reminder.
- Grading/marking every assignment

- Keeping all grading 100% current (unless you have a specific district policy regarding this)

- Pinterest-worthy lesson plans (students can still do the work if it doesn't have fancy fonts, GIFs and Bitmojis on your slide deck)

- Aesthetically pleasing themed classroom decor with only the most current student work displayed

- Classroom parties and rewards

- Laminating every single letter before you put it on a bulletin board

- Checking/grading every piece of homework

- Actually - regarding student work, how about assigning less of it? Especially if you are feeling obligated to assign it because it's what you think your administrators, or parents expect. Or you feel pressured to assign all of the same projects as your teammates. Not all classes are equal. Maybe the project you "always assign" is not a good match for your students this year. It could be a rubber ball just for this year.

- Data tracking/progress monitoring

TRIGGER WARNING - INCOMING RANT ABOUT DATA TRACKING. If repeatedly taking data from five different systems and consolidating them into another format for someone else's convenience is your favorite thing, go ahead and skip the following four paragraphs.

Let's take a little detour to discuss "progress monitoring" and its partner, the dreaded "data meeting." These two "hot" terms have been circulating in education in the United States for a while. They are fancy terms for checking your students' progress—you know, what teachers have been instinctively doing since we taught children how to read and write using sticks in the dirt.

Honestly, don't you already know how your students are performing? Have you ever been completely taken by surprise by the data? Of course, we need formative benchmark data to understand what to reteach, to whom, and how to differentiate instruction. However, the constant recrafting of summative data in spreadsheets and slides for your admin to dissect and present to "stakeholders" does not directly benefit you or your students. It is work that meets someone else's agenda.

For many teachers, these data meetings are dreaded. It goes against everything we hold dear to reduce a student to a set of numbers that can be plotted on a chart. Reducing a student to a data point is to imply that students learn and teachers teach in a vacuum. Those numbers tell us nothing about a student's social and emotional needs and their skills and growth in this area.

Ironically, we operate in an educational system that rightly demands differentiated instruction but simultaneously requires standardized tests. It isn't very objective and far from perfect. The time and energy needed for constant "data meetings" is time and energy that could be better spent. Also, during the last few years, when fully staffing schools with teachers, let alone substitutes, has been such a challenge, it's been very frustrating to spend hours compiling the data only to have meetings constantly canceled and rescheduled so that when we finally get to present the data, it is already "old news" and no longer relevant.

So yes, for me, any formal "progress monitoring" that requires me to compile in a "preferred format" data that I use every day even though it's not on a spreadsheet "snapshot" (i.e., weaponized against us to compare us with each other unfairly) is a rubber ball. I'll pick up that bounce the night before the data is due only when the meeting has been confirmed and the substitute to cover my class while I participate has been secured.

In reality, "school" is only one of the balls we need to keep in the air. We all have many other responsibilities that can fall into these broad categories:

- School
- Family
- Health/Self-Care
- Friends & Hobbies
- Spirituality

So when some school glass balls are upcoming, you know you will need to drop some rubber balls with your family responsibilities.

Suppose it's parent conference week, and you have no flexibility in your school schedule. In that case, you might need to arrange for another family member or friend to run your children to after-school activities or sports practice. When one of your children has a special event or critical game/match, you will consider that a family glass ball and something at school must be rubber. If you or a family member is sick and you need to hurriedly write lesson plans for a substitute teacher, sticking to your pacing guide and starting a new module that involves a lot of explaining just because that's what is "the next lesson in the book" may have to become a rubber ball. Assigning review work that requires minimum preparation on your behalf will be the priority. Go ahead and assign some worksheets and a video.

Students are in school for 180 days for twelve years of their life. One day of "busy work" will unlikely derail their overall education. Your family or your health need to be the glass ball.

Life in education is very dynamic. Every day, a new batch of balls is thrown at us. Now that we understand the metaphor and the mindset, let me introduce some practical tools to help you identify which priorities should be considered "glass" at different times.

Urgent and Important Are Not the Same Thing

First, it's essential to recognize that "urgent" is not the same as "important." You might receive an urgent request for data, reports, or other items. They may be "urgent" because someone else before you dropped the ball.

When I managed multiple offices and managers in the corporate world, I had a sign on my wall that reminded me, "Lack of planning on your behalf does not constitute an emergency on mine." The same can be true in education.

I can't tell you how often I had to stay late after school to compile data for some audit that the district office forgot they were having or complete pages of reports for special education professionals who had IEP or Student Study Team meeting deadlines. Of course, these things are essential. However, the fact that the professionals who often make the requests do not have 25-40 students who also need their immediate attention and engagement in front of them all day (our primary responsibility) means that last-minute requests can seem unreasonable.

Everything can seem urgent in the day-to-day running of a classroom. You may have seen a version of the meme that claims teachers make up to 1,500 decisions a day, as many as a neurosurgeon. I am still determining exactly where this data comes from, but it feels accurate.

We are constantly and instinctively reassessing and adjusting the program. Do I interrupt the flow of my teaching to redirect a student or ignore their behavior? Do I delay the start of small group instruction to play detective and unravel the playground drama that awaited me at the door after recess, or can I quickly calm students down and try to figure it out later on? Do I stop instruction if I realize some students need to get the concept or continue with the instruction until I have time to pull the students who need a reteach into a small group? It's all a constant juggling act when students are with us.

To students, everything is urgent and important. Whether it's the need for a pencil, an answer to a question, or relief from a student who is bothering them, they demand immediate attention. And, of course, not even considering fire drills, active shooter drills, tornado, earthquake, and hurricane drills, and "room clears" when an escalated student is being destructive, posing a safety threat. In the day-to-day running of a classroom, so many decisions must be made on the spot. We make so many of them automatically that we don't even notice. Often, we don't have the luxury of being intentional; we just need to react. However, decisions regarding our responsibilities outside of delivering instruction can be categorized into glass or rubber balls.

It's important to understand that just because a ball is "due tomorrow" doesn't necessarily make it a glass ball any more than a ball is rubber just because it doesn't have an "emergency" sticker on it.

The Decision Matrix

Let me give you a quick example. It's personal but will likely stay in your head as a cautionary tale, so I'm willing to share it.

About ten years ago, just after spring break, I noticed I had a mildly painful lump in a private part of my anatomy. I'll spare you the details. I was proactive in making a doctor's appointment and had to wait two weeks as I was reluctant to take a half day off school and requested the doctor's "last appointment of the day." I'm sure you know the drill. The doctor determined that the lump was a benign cyst that needed to be removed. There would likely be a two-week recovery period following the surgery. Two weeks? I couldn't conceive of taking two weeks off school! I had already used several sick days because one of my children had been ill. I asked the doctor if this was an urgent priority. She assured me that as the lump was benign, it wasn't an emergency but that it was important to take care of it.

Guess what? I was a teacher-stubborn (or teacher-martyr, which is the same thing.). I decided the surgery could wait until summer when I wouldn't have to inconvenience anyone or be stressed with planning for a substitute teacher. I justified this decision with the usual excuses we lean on to justify not using any of our "sick" days on ourselves. I had several students that year who were on behavior plans. I convinced myself they would be stressed with a substitute teacher and get into trouble. I'd be fine. I'd push through. I needed to save my sick days in case my children needed to stay home. I did not consider *my* health a glass ball. I scheduled the surgery for the very first day of summer break.

Fast forward to summer break. What had been a lump the size of a pea was now the size of a plum—and infected. It ended up being a more prolonged and more invasive surgery. The two-month recovery robbed my family and me of our entire summer. When school resumed in the fall, I still wasn't completely healed. I spent the first month of the year sitting on an inflatable donut, which is pretty hard to delicately explain to first graders who have no shame in asking you about it. I just told a white lie that I had hurt my back, but it was an embarrassment at school and parent meetings.

Turns out that small lump was a glass ball, after all. Please don't make the same mistake. Your health should always be a glass ball.

Enough said. Let's be practical.

HERE'S A SIMPLE TOOL TO SORT THROUGH OUR RESPONSIBILITIES and weed out the rubber from the glass. It's called a decision matrix, comprised of four quadrants, as shown in the graphic below. Using this tool is an excellent way to quickly clarify which tasks you should prioritize, which you should delay or delegate, and which you should strategically decide not to do (unless that reminder email shows up).

HERE IS AN EXAMPLE OF A SIMPLE DECISION MATRIX.

Your Workbook includes a full-page PDF of this matrix that you can print and use as often as you need.

This tool is often called an Eisenhower Matrix; as President Dwight Eisenhower famously said,

> What is important is seldom urgent, and what is urgent is seldom important."

The Empowered Teacher Toolkit

Clearly, Eisenhower never spent a day in a classroom! On any given day with students, we have plenty of things that are both. However, it's helpful to habitually evaluate the duties outside of delivering instruction with this tool.

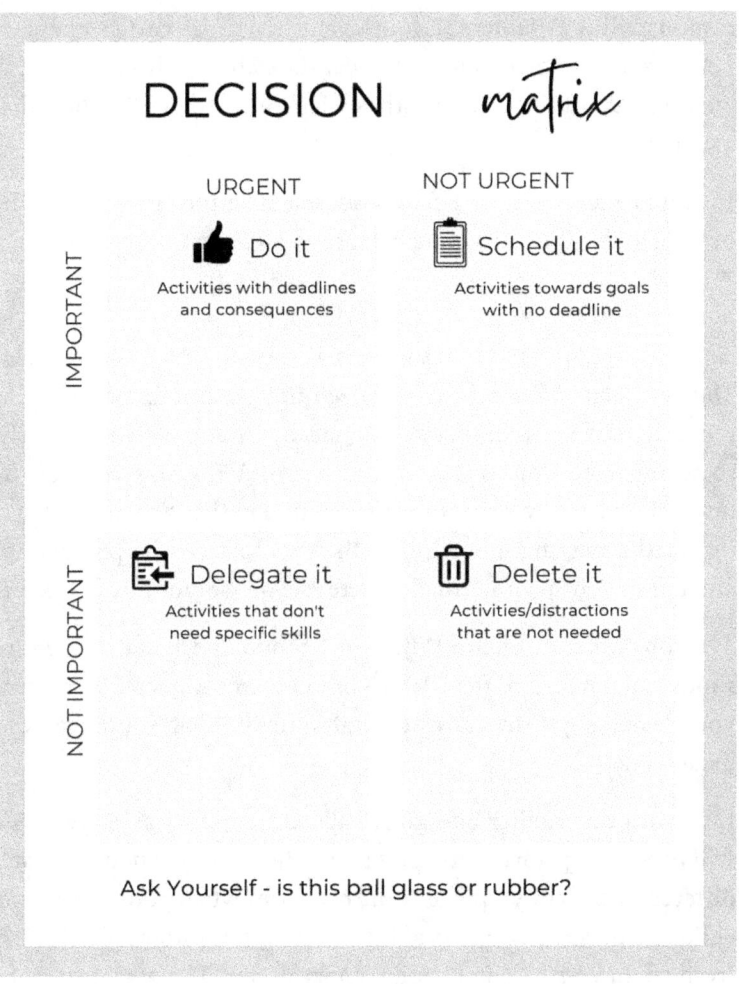

Wheel of School/Life Balance

Now that we've eliminated some balls, here's the next challenge: proactively ensuring that the remaining balls represent ALL aspects of our life beyond just our school and immediate family responsibilities. Remember our avatar from the earlier chapter? Let's make sure that some of the balls are about self-care, mental, emotional, and financial health, socializing, and yes, hobbies that bring us joy.

I created the Wheel of School/Life Balance tool to help you be proactive about maintaining balance in all aspects of your life.

THIS TOOL SHOULD BE FAMILIAR TO YOU IF YOU READ *Positive Mindset Habits for Teachers*. You need not see this information as redundant. It is a tool that should ideally be completed quarterly, so it might be time to take it out again. A full-size PDF of the instructions and worksheets can be found in the Workbook. I also included a new mini-version of the tool that can be printed out and put in your planner to complete as a quick monthly check-in.

The long version of the Wheel of School/Life Balance exercise should take no more than 10-15 minutes to complete. It can give you clear insight into any areas of your life that you have been neglecting.

Like with our rubber and glass balls, different areas of your life will become a priority in various seasons of your school year and different stages of your life. Your priorities when you have young children, daycare runs, or aging parents will differ significantly from when you are single or an empty nester. The goal is to make a habit of considering ALL of these questions regularly to ensure that you don't completely neglect any one area for an extended time.

The exercise is popular with life coaches and was originally developed by Paul J. Meyer, founder of Success Motivators Institute™. I have adapted the questions and categories to be relevant to teaching.

These are the eight areas explored in the Wheel of School/Life exercise:

- Self Care/Physical Health
- Self Care/Mental Health
- Fun Factor/Lifestyle
- Social Relations - Outside of School
- Social Relations - Inside School
- Purpose
- Personal Growth
- Financial Health

Here's how to complete the exercise.

1. For each question, score 1-10, with 10 being the highest. Think about each question, but also go with your instinct feeling of what number comes to mind. Remember, this is not an assignment you are going to have to share or get graded on! It is a tool to help you gain an understanding of where your work/life balance currently is and where opportunities for improvement may be. It is not a tool for you to beat yourself up with. It is a tool

to help you gain clarity and feel empowered to know where you should focus.

2. Once you have completed all ten questions for a domain, find the average score. Round the scores up or down accordingly.

3. Place the scores on the chart with a dot. When plotting the dots on the chart the center of the circle would be "0" and the outer ring wold be "10."

4. Connect the dots.

5. Observe your wheel and analyze the results. How does the wheel look? Is it balanced? Are there some obvious spots where scores are low?

HERE'S WHAT THE BLANK WHEEL LOOKS LIKE. AGAIN, IT WILL BE hard to write in this book, and you'll want to make a couple of copies, so grab the copy from the Workbook. If you are near a piece of paper now, you can jot down your numbers and complete the chart later.

The Empowered Teacher Toolkit

Wheel of School/Life Balance

Chart your results on this wheel for an easy visual reference to see where your life is out of balance. Chart a dot on the corresponding line number for each item (number 1 is the line closest to the center) and then connect the dots. A balanced wheel will have a nice circle towards the outer rim.

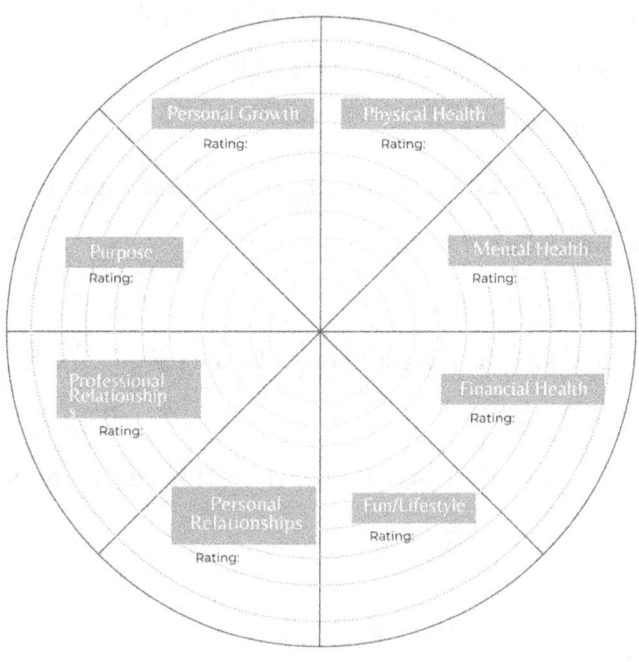

Self-Care/Physical Health

I am current with all my health check-ups, including my dentist and eye doctor.

I am a healthy weight.

I sleep without interruption 7-8 hours a night.

I eat five servings of fruits and vegetables every day.

I drink at least six glasses of water a day.

I get regular exercise.

I don't engage in excessive drinking or use of recreational drugs.

I make sure I am not sitting all day.

I take pride in my appearance.

I am happy with the way my body looks and feels.

What is your total score divided by 10? Mark it on the chart.

Self-Care/Mental Health

I set a positive intention for my day.

I catch myself when I am focusing on what I don't want and choose more productive thoughts.

I surround myself with positive people.

I am present as much as I can be during the day.

I write down three things I am grateful for every day.

I practice Brain Breaks or meditate daily.

I am mindful of my mental diet and watch TV shows/read blogs/listen to podcasts that fill me up, not deplete me and stress me out.

I limit my exposure to TV news and social media.

I read something inspirational daily, even just for a few minutes.

I practice positive mindsets and take responsibility for my own happiness.

WHAT IS YOUR TOTAL SCORE DIVIDED BY 10? MARK IT ON THE chart.

Fun Factor/Lifestyle

I feel I have enough free time to pursue leisure activities.

I have varied interests and hobbies that have nothing to do with school and students (e.g., coaching sports doesn't count).

I do at least one thing outside school every day that I enjoy.

I attend cultural events monthly.

I have a garden that I tend to or some other way to enjoy nature every day.

I take time to be playful every day with my students, my children and my pets.

I have dreams for my life, and I take time to think about them.

I leave town on vacation at least once a year.

I have an outlet for my creativity.

I read for leisure and enjoy it.

WHAT IS YOUR TOTAL SCORE DIVIDED BY 10? MARK IT ON THE chart.

SOCIAL RELATIONS (FAMILY & FRIENDS)

I engage with the family members I live with daily.

My family gets the best of me.

I talk to my family, who I don't live with, weekly.

I take responsibility for my relationship with all my family members.

There is no one in my family against whom I hold a grudge.

My relationships with my family and friends are rewarding and stress-free.

I meet/talk with my friends at least once a week.

My friends are a positive influence on my life.

My social relations leave me filled up, not depleted.

I trust my family and friends.

WHAT IS YOUR TOTAL SCORE DIVIDED BY 10? MARK IT ON THE chart.

. . .

Work Relations (Colleagues, Students & Parents)

My relationships with colleagues are rewarding and stress-free.

I enjoy my colleagues and feel connected to them.

I engage in positive conversations with colleagues, not gossiping or complaining.

I feel I can rely on and trust my colleagues and productively problem-solve with them.

I enjoy my students and feel connected to them.

I feel my students respect me.

I feel my colleagues and administrators respect me and recognize my contributions.

I feel the parents of my students respect me.

I take responsibility for my relationships at school.

I respond, not react, to challenging situations, adults, and children at school.

What is your total score divided by 10? Mark it on the chart.

Purpose

I feel my role as a teacher has a purpose.

I feel I have a positive impact on my students and my community.

I believe I play an important role in making the world a better place.

I feel connected to something greater than myself that gives me peace.

I practice intentional acts of kindness.

I strive to positively impact every situation or interaction I encounter.

I view teaching more as a calling than a career.

I take responsibility for my job satisfaction.

I feel passionate about the work I do.

I don't need external recognition or validation to feel good about what I do.

What is your total score divided by 10? Mark it on the chart.

Personal Growth

I have work/life balance.

I have a mentor who I trust.

I stretch myself by mentoring someone else.

I continue to improve my skills to be a better teacher.

I continue to learn skills that enrich my life and have nothing to do with teaching (for example, learning a new language, a new hobby, or learning to meditate).

I have goals for my life, and I am pursuing them.

I strive to be more present and joyful every day.

I am proactively learning more about myself.

I read and listen to podcasts/audiobooks for personal development, not just entertainment.

I make personal growth and increased happiness a priority.

WHAT IS YOUR TOTAL SCORE DIVIDED BY 10? MARK IT ON THE chart.

FINANCIAL HEALTH

I have three months of expenses in savings in the event of an emergency.

I carry Disability and Life Insurance through my school (if offered).

I contribute to my retirement above what is automatically deducted for my state retirement plan.

I know whom to contact when it comes time to start planning my retirement (it's never too early to plan!).

I am educated on how years of service and supplemental educational units will affect my salary if I change school districts.

I regularly invest in training and additional credentials that may increase my earning potential.

I feel my school district pays a competitive wage and that I am fairly compensated compared to other teachers.

I spend less than I make.

I have a budget that allows me to save for things I look forward to, such as vacations and fun activities.

I unsubscribe from paid services I don't use.

WHAT IS YOUR TOTAL SCORE DIVIDED BY 10? MARK IT ON THE chart.

Now you have a visual representation to help you quickly identify where you might be out of balance. Again, I recommend completing this 3-4 times a year. I also developed a quick "check-in" sheet that can be used monthly. You can find it in the Companion Workbook.

The Empowered Teacher Toolkit

School/Life Balance - Monthly Quick Check

On this worksheet, you can assess your wellbeing across multiple dimensions including: physical, emotional, spiritual, and professional. At the end of this assessment is a little box where you can note down the aspects you'd like to improve upon and how you plan to do it.

I eat healthy foods	I get enough sleep
Disagree — Neutral — Agree	Disagree — Neutral — Agree
I exercise regularly	I rest when I'm sick
Disagree — Neutral — Agree	Disagree — Neutral — Agree
I take enough time off work	I have cool hobbies
Disagree — Neutral — Agree	Disagree — Neutral — Agree
I openly talk about my problems	I spend time with my friends
Disagree — Neutral — Agree	Disagree — Neutral — Agree
I spend time with a special someone	I feel very thankful
Disagree — Neutral — Agree	Disagree — Neutral — Agree
I'm happy with my work	I work on my professional skills
Disagree — Neutral — Agree	Disagree — Neutral — Agree

What would I like to focus on this month and how:

Chapter Summary

TEACHERS HAVE AN OVERWHELMING NUMBER OF RESPONSIBILITIES and tasks that are required of them. It is a myth to think there is a magic strategy or tool to "get it all done." We need to be intentional about which tasks we choose not to do. A helpful analogy is to classify the balls we need to juggle as either glass (must do) or rubber (let them drop for now or roll away). To avoid burnout and resentment, it is also important to ensure balance in everything we are juggling. Two practical tools to help accomplish this are a Decision Matrix and the Wheel of School/Life Balance.

Get Empowered

Wys To Practice This Mindset Habit Starting Today

1 Print out the Decision Matrix. Practice using it to categorize all of the extra and pressing tasks currently lurking in your inbox or on your agenda.

2 IF YOU ARE A "LIST" PERSON, WHEN YOU MAKE YOUR LIST FOR THE day or the week, get into the habit of writing "g" or "r" next to the items (glass or rubber). Get comfortable scratching the rubber/less important items off your list without doing them. If that idea makes you uncomfortable, transfer them to a "later at some point" list. If you look at the "later" list a week or so from now, many of these items will have resolved themselves or no longer be necessary or a priority to the person who made the request.

. . .

3 COMPLETE THE WHEEL OF SCHOOL/LIFE EXERCISE. NOTICE areas of your life that you may have been neglecting. Don't use this tool to feel bad about yourself! The tool should bring awareness and clarity and help you feel empowered to make positive adjustments.

4 BASED ON THE AREAS OF DEFICIT YOU IDENTIFIED IN THE WHEEL of School/Life balance exercise, create some action items in the "Important But Not Urgent" quadrant of the decision matrix. These will likely be items pertaining to your self-care, health, personal and social relations, and maybe even finances.

5 FOCUS ON CREATING MINI HABITS THAT ARE SUSTAINABLE. Having a goal of "losing 20 pounds and getting in shape" will seem an overwhelming task, especially when school is in session. What are some important smaller habits that can get you closer to your goal? Consider eating a piece of fruit daily with your lunch instead of candy or walking during your lunch break twice a week. If finances are an issue, you could bring coffee from home instead of stopping at the coffee drive through and use the amount you save every month to pay down some debt. You could also start listening to podcasts or read books by famous money strategists such as Dave Ramsey or Suze Orman.

6 THINK CREATIVELY! WHAT ACTIVITIES COULD YOU ENGAGE IN that would help you find balance in more than one area? For example, walking at lunchtime with colleagues could help with your health and social connections.

. . .

7 Bring some of the habits for balance and self-care into your classroom. We know that much of children's social and emotional development happens at school. Activities such as practicing brain breaks, focusing on things for which we are grateful, and setting positive intentions can be practiced with students. Not only will you and your students benefit from the habits, but you will also be providing a positive role model of what balance looks like. These are things many of us wish we had been taught in school.

7

Perfect the Art of Saying "No" in a School Setting

 Ten years from now the only people who will remember how much time you spent at school will be your family."

- of unknown origin

Let's talk about setting healthy boundaries with how many hours we work.

I am aware the idea of letting balls drop is uncomfortable for many of you. There are numerous reasons why the average teacher in the United States works approximately 55 hours a week (15 hours a week or more beyond their contract). Many of those reasons are systemic. But some are also due to conditioning, unrealistic expectations, and, quite frankly, teachers' reluctance and discomfort with setting healthy boundaries.

. . .

I DEDICATED AN ENTIRE BOOK TO HOW EDUCATORS CAN SET healthier boundaries in all areas of their lives. You may find it invaluable if you want a comprehensive road map, sample scripts, mindsets, and misconceptions around saying "no" to some things and "yes" to others. It's called *Beat Teacher Burnout with Better Boundaries*, and I also offer a self-study video course with the same name. You can find details of both on my website. But for now, I will give you a quick framework and the "secret sauce" to declining requests professionally and comfortably.

LEARNING TO SAY "NO" IS NOT A SKILL WE WERE TAUGHT IN school; advocating for our needs, desires, and preferences doesn't come naturally to many of us. Most educators come to this profession because they are "helpers' and have a giving nature. It would be an over-generalization to say that we are all chronic people-pleasers and pre-conditioned to avoid conflict. Still, the profession often takes advantage of our compliant natures. As mentioned previously in this book, people will keep piling on the work until we tell them otherwise. This is not due to malicious intent; it's due to convenience.

Your administrator likely has as much on their plate as you do. A staff member who is capable, reliable, and always manages to get everything done will find themselves at the top of the administrator's list of "ideal candidates" to take on extra responsibilities or committee positions. Extra credit if that staff member is known for never saying "no."

A Crash Course in Saying "No"

First, never agree or disagree with a request to take on an extra duty or responsibility on the spot; always buy yourself some time. You are more likely to be flustered and commit to something you don't want to do if you feel rushed or obligated because the person is looking right at you.

Sample phrases to buy yourself some time are:

"Let me give that some thought and get back to you."

"Let me check my schedule and my other commitments and get back to you."

NEXT, RESPOND IN WRITING. THIS WAY, YOU WILL HAVE TIME TO gather your thoughts and a "paper trail" in the event that one becomes necessary.

Again, I offer a short story. Stories tend to stick better than suggestions. It illustrates how I learned this lesson the hard way. My principal once signed me up for a significant commitment at the district level that I had declined to his face, in person, twice. When I challenged him, he claimed he had not understood I was declining and that it was "too late" to withdraw my name.

It was a tricky situation because he had been highly insistent, almost to the point of bullying me, about me taking on this responsibility that had nothing to do with my position. I had been clear that I was not accepting the additional responsibility (again, it had nothing to do with my role at the school), but with no "paper trail" to back me up, I had no recourse. After that incident, my policy became that any time someone wanted me to participate in a committee or represent the school in any manner, I would only respond if the request were made in writing. I found it easy to blame my bad memory and say something like,

"I have a lot on my mind right now and I want to give this the attention it deserves. Please put the request in writing."

Remember, the person making the request may want to solve the problem quickly. Rather than taking the time to email you they may just walk around campus looking for another teacher who will give them a quick "yes." Problem avoided!

But let's assume you do get a request, and now it's time to answer in writing.

First, you do not owe anyone an apology. Don't use the words "sorry" or "unfortunately." Just simply state facts.

For example:

"As it turns out, I am unable to participate."

Here's the secret sauce: Give student-focused reasons for declining the request. Please don't make it about you; make it about your students and their best interests.

So, for example, don't mention that the request goes beyond your contract, that you are already overwhelmed with keeping up with your responsibilities, or that you have personal reasons (e.g., young children at home, aging parents, a partner who works nights) that would make this problematic for you. Find a reason that focuses on students. For extra impact, throw in all the education jargon you can muster. I am generally averse to using academic jargon. You may notice that this book is almost 100% void of them (by design). But likely, there are initiatives on your campus that are "hot buttons" for your administrators:

• They may be cited in your school site plans.

- They are of interest to the school board.
- They involve metrics that reflect directly on the school.

They come and go in trends, but here are some likely "hot buttons" for your administrator right now:

- data-driven instruction
- differentiated instruction
- academic rigor
- PLCs (Professional Learning Communities)
- academic proficiency as defined by state-mandated tests
- tiered intervention
- social-emotional learning
- trauma-informed teaching practices
- skill remediation

So, when drafting a student-focused reason for your decline, throw in some "hot buttons."

Here are some examples:

"As you may be aware, this is my first year in this particular grade assignment. I owe it to my students to spend any additional time I have gaining a firmer grasp of the required curriculum so that I can best support their academic success."

"THIS YEAR, I FIND MYSELF IN A CHALLENGING SITUATION WHERE many of my students struggle with the skills they need to succeed in this grade. I will be dedicating any extra time I have to develop and implement interventions that help remediate their academic deficiencies."

. . .

"As you may remember, we had a lot of turnover in this grade span this year, and I am now the senior member of the team. I am obliged to devote much of my extracurricular time to training the new teachers on specific lesson planning, data collection, assessments, and interventions that we use. This area of responsibility should be my main focus to ensure the success of all students in this grade."

Let's review the steps to declining requests in a professional, student-focused way.

1 Buy yourself some time (no immediate response either way)

2 Answer the response in writing

3 Don't feel the need to apologize

4 Give a student-focused reason

5 Wish the person well with their event/committee/initiative

Saying "Yes" With Limitations

So that's how to say "no" if someone asks you to take on an extra duty. What if it's a duty that it is assumed you automatically have? Here are the best strategies:

1. Give as much notice to succession planning/transition time as possible.

For example, let's say you always put on 8th grade promotion as you are the only 8th grade teacher. What if your child is graduating high school that year or has their 8th-grade promotion at a different school? Usually, those promotions all happen on the same day, and, of course, going to your child's event should be a priority. You will feel more comfortable and will be more successful if you give your administrator notice right at the beginning of the year that they will need to find someone else to take on the role.

2. OFFER TO "TRAIN" YOUR REPLACEMENT OR SPLIT THE responsibilities with someone else. For example, you could take on a lesser role of helping with the organization but not be responsible for the last-minute details and being present at the event.

You could take on a lesser role for one year or semester while you train your replacement. Remember, the reason for extra duties is your administrator needs to accomplish something without their involvement. The easier you make it for them, the more likely they will agree that you will take on a lesser role or eliminate your participation in the duty altogether.

3. SET STRICT LIMITATIONS TO YOUR INVOLVEMENT. THIS WILL BE the strategy for a duty that is technically part of your responsibility. You may not be able to ditch the duty, but you can set some boundaries that will make the duty less time and energy-consuming or less painful. Consider these limitations like accommodations for students taking tests. They still need to take the test, but we can set them up so they will be less stressed and more successful with accommodation. I am suggesting that you advocate for some accommodations of your own.

Here are some examples of saying yes, but with limitations.

School event supervision: "I can help supervising the science fair next Wednesday, but I'll need to leave by 6 PM to catch my son's soccer practice."

Committee involvement: "I can serve on the curriculum committee again this year, as long as meetings are scheduled during my planning periods so I don't have to stay after school."

Academic coaching: "I'm happy to help coach the math team this semester, but I won't be available for competitions or events outside of our regular Wednesday meeting time from 3–4 PM."

Peer mentoring: "I'm willing to mentor a new teacher, as long as we limit meetings to 30 minutes per week during my prep period on Thursdays."

Remember to advocate for what you need to make whatever event/committee you are on successful. How well an event goes (especially one that parents or board members are invited to) reflects directly on the school, and an administrator should be motivated to give you what you need to make the school and, by default, them look good.

For example, you are a music teacher, and your administrator has requested that you put on a concert at the last minute.

"In order to make an event that we can all be proud of, I will need to get a substitute to cover my regular class for two days so that I can dedicate all my time to the preparations. Also, I need your support in conveying to the general education teachers that I won't be able to move classes around to accommodate teacher preferences once I publish a rehearsal schedule."

If an administrator asks you to move heaven and earth and you feel you can't say "no," then at least get comfortable requesting accommodations to support your success.

Chapter Summary

Teachers work too many hours. We need to get comfortable declining requests to protect our energy and avoid burnout. The secret to doing so professionally is to state a student-focused reason. Taking inventory of all the additional duties we have taken on and evaluating them based on our passion for them is an excellent habit. Many additional responsibilities may technically be considered "part of our job," in which case we need to be proactive about setting limitations on our involvement and advocating for accommodations to make the duties less burdensome.

Get Empowered

Ways to Practice This Mindset Habit Starting Today

1 Conduct an Extra Duty Inventory using the exercise in the Workbook. Make a list of adjunct duties you currently have and will be asked (or assumed) to take on again next year. Evaluate them based on how much or how little passion you have for them. Does coaching, mentoring, tutoring, or being on a particular committee feel like "the good stuff," or does it leave you drained and dreading every time you need to participate?

2 ONCE YOU HAVE YOUR LIST, DECIDE WHICH ADJUNCT DUTIES YOU have the flexibility to decline next year or proactively resign from. You may be unable to decline duties mandated by contract

or closely aligned with the subject you teach, such as science camp if you are a science teacher or putting on concerts if you are a music teacher. But I bet there is at least one other item that you could ditch of you summoned up the courage to try.

3 DRAFT SAMPLE EMAILS USING A STUDENT-FOCUSED REASON as the reason for declining or resigning from the assigned duty. If it is a duty that you cannot decline or resign from, draft emails where you emphasize your commitment but suggest limitations to your involvement. Again, make the reason and focus of your limitations be about the success of the duty/mission, not about you or your lack of time. Use the tips, strategies, and scripts in this chapter to help.

8

Be Intentional About Your Narrative

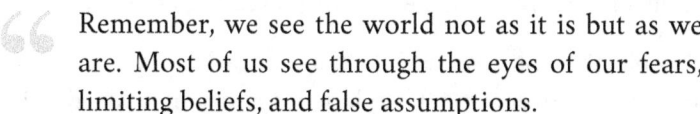
Remember, we see the world not as it is but as we are. Most of us see through the eyes of our fears, limiting beliefs, and false assumptions.

- Robin Sharma, author of *The Monk Who Sold His Ferrari*

IN ORDER TO HAVE A MORE POSITIVE TEACHING EXPERIENCE, WE need to passionately and proactively protect our peace. We must protect our peace from pervasive negative narratives about teaching, toxic school practices, parents, and coworkers.

That may sound harsh, but we need to take charge if we want to be happier and end our day with enough energy to engage with other people and activities we love.

When protecting our peace becomes a priority, so many things about our lives change for the better. But it's not a "one and done" proposition. It's intentional work that only we can do, and it's a lifetime endeavor. Internal peace isn't something that we can buy at the store. It does show up at our door with Amazon

Prime delivery. We need to do the work. And this chapter can help.

Let's start by revisiting one of my Four Pillars- Other teachers' experiences don't need to be your experience. What does that mean, exactly?

Examining Your Teaching Story

What are the stories that you tell yourself about teaching? That it gets more challenging every year? That students are getting less engaged and more difficult to manage every day? That students and parents lack respect for our time and what we do? That certainly may be true in some circumstances, but not in all.

As a whole, the collective narrative about teachers in N. America is that we are overworked, underpaid, and undervalued. This narrative is reinforced by social media memes, jokes, and teachers as they commiserate and exchange war stories in staff rooms and meetings. Again, I am not saying these things aren't true in general. Teaching is tough. Education is facing a lot of challenges. But does this need to be true in your experience? Not necessarily. You have the power to be proactive, elicit different responses from different situations, and ultimately, create your own experience. Some teachers out in the world still have passion, energy, creativity, and love being with their students every day. I'm willing to bet a couple of them are on your campus. Honestly, I was one of them for the better part of twenty years. But it didn't happen without effort on my part and vigilance to not fall victim to the collective narrative.

Consider this. Have you ever had a student you dreaded coming up through the grades to your class? It's happened to me so many times.

One teacher, in particular, made a point of telling me about this student or that, how awful they were, and how much I should hope they didn't end up in my class. Whenever we passed each other in the hall or on the way in or out of the cafeteria, she'd tell me, "Just you wait, this is the worst class I've ever had!" Seriously, I think she told me that five years in a row. Her classroom was next to mine, and I often shuddered as I could hear her yelling through the walls—good grief, what a miserable experience for her and her class.

Every time she said this, I would smile and say the same thing, "Maybe they'll mature by next year!" I hoped she'd get the hint that I wouldn't get roped into a complaining session. And every year, low and behold, the class I inherited was overall just fine. We created a great community of respect and collaboration, we had fun, and everyone learned. Of course, there were a few challenging students, and not every day was a party. But on the whole, the class bore little resemblance to the class of disrespectful delinquents the other teacher had described.

I'M SURE YOU HAVE SIMILAR STORIES OF STUDENTS WHO YOU experienced in a completely different way than another teacher did. Part of that has to do with my first Pillar - Our energy teaches more than our lesson plans. A chronically overwhelmed, resentful, and negative teacher will not bring out the best in students. When students feel seen, respected, and part of a strong classroom community with a calm and consistent teacher, of course, they will bring a better version of themselves to class.

But another aspect of this is that we often create the experience we expect to have. At the risk of sounding like a bumper sticker, **we get what we expect.**

. . .

You may be familiar with this parable. Two young men were looking to move from one village in China to another. The first young man went to the elder in the new village and asked, "What are the people like in this village?" The elder asked in return, "What are the people like where you come from?" The young man said, "Oh, they are great! They are kind and helpful." The elder smiled and reassured the young man, "You will find that the people here are kind and helpful, too."

The second young man went to the elder and asked the same question. Again, the elder asked him, "What are the people like where you come from?" The second young man replied, "They're awful! That's why I want to leave. They are cruel and greedy." The elder looked at the second young man and replied, "You will find that the people here are also greedy and cruel."

This story reinforces Robin Sharma's quote from the beginning of this chapter. We see and experience the world as we are. In psychology this is called a "self fulfilling prophecy." Here's how it can play out at school - if we expect to have an awful class or a terrible parent-teacher conference, we will. If we already have a preconceived notion that something will be difficult, it will be. Could it be that the saying is true? Do you get what you expect?

Although that may sound overly simplistic to some of you, the idea is validated by brain science. We'll dig into this a little deeper. However, the first step to rewriting your teaching narrative is to recognize that you get to have your own experience of people and situations. One teacher's "worst class ever" is another teacher's dream class. One teacher's "hell grade" is another teacher's favorite grade to teach.

So step one - tune out the noise, and decide to have your own experience.

Retune Your Satellite Radio

Step two is to retune your satellite. Are you familiar with satellite radio in your car? Hundreds of channels are available in all genres. They are all equally available to everyone, all the time. Yet to listen to one, we have to tune in. Set the dial.

Despite hundreds of options, most people listen to the same two or three channels out of habit, comfort, or just lack awareness that other channels are available to them.

So, what channel have you set your tuner to? The "Good Things Happen in my Classroom" channel, or the "I Can Barely Make it Through the Day" channel?

Are you setting your radar and your intention to notice things that you want or things that you don't want?

Are you talking about possibilities and solutions to issues, or are you complaining, commiserating with other burned-out teachers, and feeling powerless to improve anything?

Which songs are stuck in our head?

HERE'S THE RUB: MANY PEOPLE REACT AUTOMATICALLY TO WHAT IS happening around them. They are unaware that they have a choice about what they notice, what they think, and, therefore, how they feel. They don't realize that they have the power to change the channel.

. . .

MOST OF US UNDERSTAND THAT THERE ARE MANY THINGS WE DO unconsciously. First of all, body functions. We don't need to think about breathing, digesting food or the sequence of events that need to happen to fire up our muscles to walk or kick a ball. Next, there are actions that we have performed so many times that we have "muscle memory" around them. For example, brushing our teeth, driving a car, riding a bike. There are neurological processes that allow us to remember the motor skills in order to perform these tasks with little conscious effort. Think about the times you have pulled up in your driveway in your car and realized you weren't even paying attention to how you got home.

But not everyone realizes the extent to which our unconscious beliefs, conditioning, biases, and past experiences determine what we notice in our experiences and, therefore, what we tune into.

Consider this. At any given instant, our brain must process tens of thousands of pieces of sensory input. Sights, sounds, smells, physical sensations, tastes. We are not able to simultaneously process all these pieces of information with our conscious minds. The brain, in many ways seeks patterns. So, when we experience a situation, our brain will find things that confirm our views, beliefs, and values when filtering the things we notice. Unconsciously, we either don't notice things or we distort the input to confirm our beliefs. In the psychological literature, this is called confirmation bias.

HERE'S HOW IT COULD PLAY OUT AT SCHOOL. YOU NOTICE TWO students bump into each other in the hall. If your experience of them is that they are both easy-going, low-maintenance students, you will likely assume it was an accident. But if your experience of one of the students has been that they exhibit attention-seeking or aggressive behavior, you will assume that the act was intentional and that one student is to blame. You will interpret the incident in a way that confirms what you already believe to be true about the student. "There they go again!"

IN ADDITION TO ALL OF THE AUTOMATIC FILTERING, OUR BEAUTIFUL brain, when cruising along automatically, tends to have a negativity bias. This means that even if two events of the same intensity occur, a negative experience will significantly affect our brain and overall emotional state more than a positive experience. Researchers also claim that of the average 50 - 60,000 thoughts we have daily, 70 - 80% tend to be negative. That crappy radio channel is hardwired in our DNA.

FROM AN EVOLUTIONARY STANDPOINT, HAVING A BRAIN constantly looking out for danger and tuning into the "What Could Go Wrong" channel played a vital component of our survival. Focusing on the negative helped us stay alive. Researchers have identified more than one hundred cognitive biases, most of which are unconscious. If we want to tune into another station, we need to be mindful of our unconscious beliefs and conditioning and intentional about rewriting the collective narrative about teaching.

In *Positive Mindset Habits for Teachers*, I did a deep dive into the latest research on happiness. The bad news is that our brains developed to keep us safe, not necessarily to make us happy. But the good news is this: we can adopt many intentional habits that can help us improve our happiness quotient and tune into the "I'll Notice More of What I Like" channel. I termed this perspective becoming a "Joy Detective." We need to retrain ourselves to focus on what we want and keep what we don't want in perspective.

LET'S SEE IF THIS EXAMPLE RESONATES. HOW OFTEN HAVE YOU LET your mood and your day be dominated and derailed by the two to three students competing for the title of class clown? Of course, the behavior needs to be dealt with; we can't just pretend it's not happening. But what about the other 25 students in the class who were on task and productively collaborating and focusing on their work? When you consider your class as a whole and go home and talk to your family about your students, which group do you focus your attention on? The majority who are being compliant, or the minority who are driving you nuts and wearing you out?

Quick reminder: none of this chapter (or anything I say anywhere in the book) is meant to make you feel shame or guilt. If you realize that you have been more negative than desirable, it's not your fault. Not only are we navigating one of the most challenging careers, but we are also working against a collective negative narrative around teaching, against a very disaster-focused culture, and, if that weren't enough, we're working against our biology. Tuning into a different channel isn't necessarily easy, but it will be worth it.

So, what strategies can help? Let's look at a few.

Becoming Aware of Your Story

First, with awareness comes choice. I say that a lot because it's true. The cognitive tendencies I described above were unconscious. If we never question what we believe and what we notice, we will remain unconscious. So, let's uncover your beliefs about teaching.

The Companion Workbook has an exercise to help you define your beliefs about teaching. Maybe you've completed an exercise similar to this before. Either way, it is worth repeating as our beliefs are constantly changing. Most educators, for better or worse, have a different perspective on teaching since the global pandemic where so much that we believed to be a constant about schooling (i.e., it takes place in person, in a classroom) was turned upside down.

If you struggle to define your beliefs about education, here are some sentence starters to help. They are also on the Workbook pages.

I think students, in general, are …

I think parents, in general, are …

I think other teachers are …

I think teaching, in general, is …

I think my administrator is …

I think my district/central office is …

I think what other people in my life think about teaching is …

I believe I am this type of teacher …

I believe teaching CAN be …

Analyze

Invest some time in analyzing your answers to these questions. In general, which radio station are these beliefs tuned into? Is it the "I Don't Know if I Can Make it Until Retirement?" channel or the "I Make a Positive Impact" channel? Here's a clue—any time we generalize or use absolutes such as "all, always, never, no one," it should be a clue that we are working with limiting beliefs.

REFRAME BELIEFS BASED ON WHAT IS RESOURCEFUL.

As we discussed above, our brains find a way to look for evidence to validate what we believe. So, evaluating beliefs to see if they are "true" is not always helpful. Our biases will find a way to notice what makes them true. So we want to evaluate our beliefs to see whether or not they are **resourceful**. Does believing that we are powerless to control student behavior help us? No. Go back to the idea of growth mindset. Does the idea that we're not good learners and that learning is boring and difficult help us? Of course not. So it makes sense to REFRAME any of our beliefs that don't serve us and to adopt beliefs that are helpful in our quest for a more positive and peaceful experience. But how?

THE TWO EASIEST WAYS TO HELP US REFRAME OUR BELIEFS ARE:

One: intentionally seek evidence that goes against your unresourceful belief (I promise you, it's there!)

Two: always stick with facts, not knee-jerk reactions and internal "creative storytelling".

SEEK CONTRARY EVIDENCE

Stories stick, folks. So I am going to give you two examples of how to seek contrary evidence. The second example will be in a school setting, this first one about dating. Yep. Let's do it.

At age 46, I found myself unexpectedly single. I met my husband when I was young and married early, so when I was suddenly thrown into the dating world mid-life, I was overwhelmed and lacked the mindset and skills required to create positive experiences. I tried a dating website, and my first few encounters were pretty discouraging. Before I knew it, I had adopted a whole lot of limiting beliefs about online dating.

Unconsciously, I knew better than to massively generalize by saying, "All single men are..." But I sure started many conversations with my friends: "Most single men on apps are...." I joined an online group of more mature female daters, and the focus was heavily on how not to fall prey to scammers. Sure enough, my radar when evaluating profiles was more set on rooting out who was embellishing their online profile (lying) and scamming than who had the potential to be a respectful and supportive partner. I also had my mom's voice (in my head and real-life) constantly telling me, "No one wants a woman over 50, you'd better hurry up and not let yourself go."

Sure enough, whenever I opened up men I was "matched" with, I would notice profile after profile of men in their 50's and 60's who only wanted to date women under 45.

A few months in, I was contacted by I started an online an "international antique dealer." He was charming, handsome, well traveled. I did my due diligence So I thought!). His business had an excellent website. He called, wrote long emails, and sent virtual flowers. He was on an international trip and even called from "overseas" a few times.

After a few months of him traveling to pick out new antiques, we were all set to meet and spend New Years eve together. I was so excited. He'd sent me pictures of hist first class ticket (impressive!) Just before he was supposed to board the plane, he emailed me desperately needing $5400. He claimed he needed to pay import taxes on some antiques. They had been impounded at customs due to "changed laws." He was stuck at the airport on his way to me, his credit card was already maxed out with tariffs; he'd pay me back as soon as he met me. His plea included photos of what seemed to be a fake passport and fake custom tariff receipts. I wasn't wholly blindsided (there had been red flags along the way), but I was so disappointed and ashamed. Even though I had not given him money or inappropriate personal information, I had invested plenty of time and energy in him. My heart hurt for other vulnerable, trusting women who would fall for his ploy. I did some more searching on Google for his image, name, and profile (let's find more evidence! Let's prove I'm right about these rapscallions!). Sure enough, I found a forum devoted to this scammer and his many aliases. The stories of women who had lost money they didn't have to spare were heartbreaking and numerous.

I have so many more dating stories like this. In retrospect, some of them are funny. Stories of my dating exploits were crowd-pleasers in the staff lunchroom (beats complaining about students). The constant repetition of these stories only reinforced my limiting beliefs more. Men on dating sites aren't relationship material. They're charming on dates because they spend all their time dating, not in relationships. They all want younger women. They all lie on their profiles. Yep, I had some stinking thinking!

WHY AM I SHARING THIS STORY WITH YOU? FIRST, I WILL USE IT TO explain how I turned this situation around. Then, to illustrate that the positive mindset habits in this book can help you in every aspect of your life, not just teaching. Any area of your life can benefit from you taking the time to identify, question, and possibly reframe your beliefs surrounding it, whether it is relationships, parenting, money, spiritual growth or your ability to learn new skills and successfully apply them.

So, how did I turn this turbulent, negative dating cycle around?

First, I took a step back. I put myself on a dating hiatus. I had been on many first and second dates, and the common denominator in all these dates was me. I had enough self-awareness to realize that my attitude was not only crappy but unhelpful. I decided to question my own beliefs. I challenged myself to make some lists.

1 I listed all the people I know who are happily in long-term relationships and marriages. That list had 20+ names on it in less than five minutes!

2 I listed all the happy couples I knew who had met online or through dating apps. That list had four weddings just in my family.

3 I listed all the dates I had been on where the men were charming and truthful but not at the same season of life as me, or having the same relationship goals. Honestly, men who were great for someone, just not great for me. That list comprised about 75% of the men I had dated.

As soon as I stepped back enough to look at evidence contrary to my limiting beliefs, the evidence was everywhere. The vast majority of people who are dating online are authentic. Most people are seeking someone in their age bracket with similar relationship goals. Just because someone isn't perfect for me doesn't mean they aren't ideal for someone. At least four of the men I dated have since gotten married. The ads didn't lie - plenty of lovely people are finding their match on Match.com.

. . .

I REALIZED I NEEDED TO RECALIBRATE MY SATELLITE SIGNAL. Instead of scanning the airwaves for scammers and haters, I needed to scan for helpers and lovers. I needed to look for what I liked about people, not what I didn't like. I needed to screen in, not screen out.

I rewrote my dating story on paper and in my mind. I set my intention that when I went on a date, I would focus on finding three things that I liked about a person. Shortly after, a few months after my 50th birthday (take that, Mom!) I met a quiet, thoughtful widower. He is everything I ever dreamed of in a partner and much more. We are nine years into our beautiful relationship and counting. When people ask how we met, I hesitate for an instant, wanting to say "at farmer's market." My guy just confidently says, "on-line dating." He'd been tuned into the right station all along and only had a positive experience. Go figure.

Stick with the Facts

Part two of reframing limiting beliefs sounds too simplistic to be effective, but you'd be surprised how often we gloss over it. That is the practice of asking ourselves, *"Is that true?"* When we have created some complete story in our heads and feel our emotions spiral out of control, we need to stop, breathe, and ask ourselves, *"What are the actual facts of this situation?"*

Has this ever happened to you? Just as the morning bell is about to ring, you quickly check your email and see a message from your administrator asking, "Please stop by my office after school when you have a chance?" Or from a parent requesting that we call them after school. Suddenly, your beautiful brain, evolved to be hypervigilant to danger, is off and running, creating an imaginary scenario of impending doom and disaster. You imagine the worst. You have rehearsed conversations in your head, what you'll say, what the other person will say. Before you know it, your body is having a physical stress response to something that not only isn't happening but, in all likelihood, won't happen. When you get to the end of the day and nervously approach your administrator, they simply want your opinion on a new resource they are considering. The parent just wanted to drop off some class supplies or know when they can drop by with treats for their child's birthday.

I hate it when I start spiraling into scary imagined futures! It can be avoided by stopping, taking a breath, and asking, "What are the facts of this situation?" The fact is that your boss wants to talk to you when you have time. That's it. That's all you know. Maybe they want to thank you for doing a great job and are giving you a day off. (Sorry, I got lost in a fantasy there myself. I mean to say a " giving you a free jeans pass.")

NOTE: IF YOU ARE AN ADMINISTRATOR READING THIS, CAN I ASK A favor? Please save your staff a day's worth of acid stomach by adding half a sentence to your email. "Please stop by my office when you get a chance *so that we can discuss*...(complete the sentence as necessary)." It could be something innocuous, such as science camp details or next year's curriculum. It might be a little more stressful, such as " How can I support you with the (specific student's or parent's name)?" But in any event, please tell people why you want to meet with them. We know you are all so busy. We assume it will be something negative if you're taking the time to meet with us.

. . .

In my book *Teaching in the Post-Covid Classroom*, I shared a story about having anxiety whenever I interacted with a particular principal. I was brand new to a very high-performing school. I was really in culture shock, to be honest. Everyone on campus seemed to have drunk the crazy Kool-Aid and worked at least 60 hours a week. The admin and vice principal were mandated to have three coaching days a week. This meant they toured classrooms unannounced, with clipboards and multiple rubrics. On several occasions, I never received any feedback after the visit. So the vibe was less "coaching" and more micro-managing and policing. The district had a very long list of rigid rules regarding how they liked things done, right down to the academic discourse students (called "scholars") should use in class. As an example, one of my colleagues got called in to discuss why part of her learning objective for the lesson had been erased from the board. Turns out she had been reading to the class in a swivel chair and when she turned her arm had erased part of it and she hadn't noticed it. Crazy stuff like that. It was like teaching in a pressure cooker.

To make things worse, one veteran staff member decided to informally "take me under their wing." She kept warning me to "watch out." I was untenured, and she told me that once this administrator found something he didn't like about a person, he had no qualms about not renewing their contract. Remember, it was a happier pre-pandemic time when teachers were still in good supply for well-paying districts. And this was a very high-paying district within walking distance of my house. It was my dream job. I was a single parent with two children who were still in college and on my healthcare plan. I could not afford to mess up this opportunity. Every day, various staff members would share new examples of this administrator's ridiculous demands and inflexibility.

I was a bundle of nerves and started second-guessing myself anytime I interacted with him. I had bought into the narrative that he was a ridiculous stickler with zero tolerance for anything done in any way other than how he would do it. Ok, he was a little extreme. He even dictated which "call and response" we should use. He was highly focused on student achievement data and strictly enforced a "no class parties" policy for even landmark days such as Halloween. Did I mention it was an elementary school? I don't think letting tiny "scholars" have a little fun was not going to scar them for life academically.

But he wasn't a tyrant "out to get" new staff members. No. How could that possibly benefit him?

One day, after a lunch period spent sobbing and huddled in a supply closet for privacy, I decided something had to change. I needed to stop being a victim. I followed my advice and wrote down the facts of my relationship with this administrator.

First, he hired me without an interview. I had missed a recruitment fair due to an overseas trip but had submitted video responses to standard questions. He was "so confident" in me that he hired me sight unseen. On the day I showed up to pick up keys, he walked me to my empty classroom, ran through a list of things I might need even down to asking if I wanted desks or flexible seating. When I returned to campus the next day, everything had been delivered to my room. Three weeks into school, when I nervously told him I would be more comfortable teaching with a document camera than the current tech setup, he put in a tech request for me right away. After an unscheduled visit to my classroom, he wrote a note complimenting me on having the scholars work collaboratively in small groups. After my first formal observations, he gave me positive feedback and constructive suggestions for growth. When I looked at the facts, not the story that was spiraling in my imagination, this administrator had been completely efficient and supportive. Did we have the same communication style? Not at all. Ultimately, did that matter? Also, not at all.

Looking back at it now, I'm a little embarrassed. I should have known better than to be influenced into believing that having a bad experience with him was a forgone conclusion. My experience of him did not necessarily need to be the same as other teachers' experience of him. Had I looked, I would have found many teachers on campus who liked working for him. They appreciated that he was highly structured, organized, and clear with his expectations. There was no guessing where you stood with him. He was highly reliable. If you weren't five minutes early to a meeting, you were already late. It was pretty crazy, but hey, we wrapped up on time!

At the end of the year, this administrator accepted a director position in another school district. Before he left, he advocated for me at the district level. A new school was opening, and my teaching position had been eliminated. He told me he respected me and did not want the school to lose such a great teacher, and he arranged for me to move to a different grade rather than be transferred to a different school.

Would it have been better for him to have told me all these positive things at the time? Sure, he certainly had some communication quirks that he could improve on. But truthfully, I learned more from him than any other administrator I have ever worked with, even though we only worked together for a year.

Chapter Summary

Our teaching experience doesn't need to be the same as other people's; we get to create our own. It's essential to recognize what "music station" is playing in our head and to redirect our thoughts and focus accordingly.

Once we become aware of our limiting beliefs about a person or a situation, we can train ourselves to move beyond our cognitive biases and reframe those thoughts into a more positive and empowering narrative.

Get Empowered

Ways To Practice This Mindset Habit Starting Today

1 Complete the Limiting Beliefs About Education exercise in the Workbook. Evaluate your beliefs in terms of whether they are resourceful or not and if they get you closer to your goal of a more positive teaching experience. Don't evaluate them on whether or not they are "true." True for others does not need to be true for you. Plus, our brain is going to find a way to find evidence for what we believe is true.

2 TAKE OUT A SHEET OF PAPER. WRITE OUT A *NEW STORY* OF YOUR educational career, focusing on all the things you have enjoyed, the positives, and the passionate and professional people you have worked with. Is teaching challenging? Heck, yes! Is it possible to still find purpose and passion in teaching? Also, heck yes! Tell yourself that story. Set your satellite to that radio station, and notice everything in your day that supports that.

. . .

3 SEEK TO BECOME MORE AWARE OF THE ENERGETIC RADIO STATION people are tuned into. What conversations are they having? What are they choosing to notice (consciously or unconsciously), and what are they ignoring? What's playing in your staff room? What's playing at your grade span, departmental, or leadership meetings? Are people tuned into the "This is tough, but let's try and figure it out" channel or the "Let's complain about the problem until we feel defeated and hopeless" channel? I will address how to deal with toxically negative people and environments in the next chapter. But for now, just become aware. Remember, with awareness comes choice.

9

Proactively Protect Your Peace

> Daring to set boundaries is about having the courage to love ourselves, even when we risk disappointing others.

Brene Brown - Author & Researcher

Here's a story. In retrospect, I find pretty amusing. However, I found it confusing and hurtful at the time and wasn't sure how to respond without sounding defensive.

One day before school, I was in our staff room checking my mailbox and making some copies. I had my nice fresh cup of coffee in my hand. Rather than squirrel away my Keurig machine in my classroom, I had put it in our tiny kitchen for everyone to use. Actually, "kitchen" is a bit of an overstatement. It was a small room with a sink, a thirty-year-old fridge that hadn't been defrosted (ever), and two old microwaves that, if used at the same time, blew the circuit breaker. Anyway, there I was, living my best teacher life, copies under my arm, coffee in my hand, and hoping to get a chance to take a few sips before it went cold when a co-worker passed by me and said,

"Your cheerfulness is offensive to me. And I'm not the only one."

My cheerfulness? I wracked my mind. Was I singing Disney tunes out loud? Had I been smiling and talking to the birds on my way across the playground? In fairness, those are things that I do on the regular. Those are things I do on the regular. But not out loud. And I certainly have more sense than to do them at 7:15 AM around teachers who have just commuted for an hour and have yet to find their way to that Keurig machine. Worst of all, did I have the audacity to share a positive statement about a student or say something I was looking forward to in my classroom that day? Nope. All I had said was, "Good morning!"

The accusation stung. "How exactly am I cheerful?" I asked.

The answer: "You are all smiley and shiny and not complaining."

Well, friends, that's how low the bar was on our campus. The only thing you had to do to be considered "offensively cheerful" was to not complain to everyone, at any time of the day, whenever you ran into them.

It seems we had collectively taken "commiserating" and "admiring problems" (complaining about legitimate things but with no openness to consider solutions) to an Olympic sport level.

While the Pollyanna "stick a smiley face bandaid on it" toxically positive school culture is damaging, a toxically negative culture is worse. Optimism and proactivity are not naturally contagious, but negativity spreads like a California wildfire on a hot, windy day.

. . .

So here's the reality: none of us teach in a vacuum. There are students, of course. With students, we can close our doors and become revolutionary, acting as cheerful as we please. But what about the rest of the interactions we encounter throughout our day?

Parents, other teachers, administrators, coaches, and school support staff are all relationships we need to navigate. If we want a more positive experience in teaching and life, we need to be proactive about protecting our emotional environment.

Negative and drama-focused people tend to play their radio station very loudly, and it can be easy for their station to drown out ours. We must be mindful of how easy it is to get drawn into other people's energy and take proactive steps to protect our peace. Otherwise, we'll end up with those songs stuck in our heads. Here we are again. The answer is boundaries and getting comfortable setting them with people who drain our energy.

Unsubscribe From the Drama

Please understand that I am not shaming negative people. As challenging as education is, everyone is negative once in a while. There certainly is a lot to complain about that is valid, and we all need at least one teaching "bestie," who acts as our safe place to vent to and cry with. Your bestie is that friend who knew you were crying in a fetal position under your desk during lunch and gives you your space but sends over a student with emergency chocolate and a love note when lunch is over. And then runs to your room after school to hear all about what upset you and make you laugh.

. . .

There is a big difference between having a bad day (which happens occasionally to everyone) and having a bad attitude.

We all have bad days and challenging students and situations. But there is a vast difference between those colleagues who listen to us, laugh and cry with us, and help us feel better and energized, and those who are constantly negative, complain and drain us.

I call the first group of people "battery chargers." We feel better when we've been around them. The latter group is made of "battery drainers." These are the chronically negative people who suck any joy right out of us. Often engaging with them for even just a few minutes leaves us walking away slower, stooped over, and in need of a stiff drink. Sometimes aptly called "energy vampires," these are the people with whom we need to set a boundary.

Remember, boundaries are about *our* behavior. We are not going to change anybody else. It is not productive to "call people out" on their constant negativity. Their energy and how they experience life is their responsibility.

For the most part, chronic complainers are reactive people who see adverse circumstances as constantly happening to them. They have much work to do to reframe their paradigm and see how their energy worsens their situation. Pointing this out to them is unlikely to be effective or well-received.

Again, please support colleagues experiencing a bad day or week or a particularly challenging class. However, you must set healthy boundaries with colleagues who never have a positive word to say about any student, parent, class, or experience. You know in your gut who they are.

Here's how I like to look at it. Do you ever find yourself low-key annoyed when you get emails from the same vendor you haven't shopped with for months or years? Maybe it's just once a week, so you just hit "delete" without opening it, but under the surface, you are a little irritated every time. Scroll to the email's end and hit "unsubscribe." It takes an extra 20 seconds or so, but compared to 20 seconds now to a few seconds of irritation again and again, unsubscribing makes more sense in the whole scheme of things. And it's the same for the energy vampires. We must find a way to "unsubscribe" from their drama by quietly minimizing our contact with them.

Here are a few ideas to help you.

First, if the staff room at lunch is the unofficial congregation ground of energy vampires (misery loves company), you may need to find a way to make your copies and heat your coffee at a time when you have the room to yourself. If that's impossible, a good strategy is to be on your mobile phone when you pass through so that no one engages you. It doesn't even need to be a real conversation, if you get my drift. Pretending to be on hold for someone is a plausible strategy.

I don't usually advocate avoidance as a strategy, but I see no benefit to confronting people in this case. Of course, you can pull up a chair to the lunch table, but be sure not to get dragged into complaining. If I were in the staffroom at lunch, I would try to share something funny that had happened in the classroom. I knew that sharing student successes could sound braggy (maybe "aggressively cheerful"), but there was always something funny to share.

If you find a negative staffroom vibe rubbing off on you, creating a more positive lunchtime routine for yourself could be the best solution. One of my professors in college only ever referred to a teacher's staff lounge as "a den of iniquity." Having never been in one, I thought that was a gross exaggeration. Twenty years later, I can see why he came to that conclusion.

When the Drama is a Teammate

What if one of your teammates is always negative? You will need to find a professional and productive way to work with them. Avoidance is not an option.

The best way to accomplish this is to set meeting times and norms. In my last position, I taught fourth grade with two other teachers. We were in different buildings and didn't have a common prep period. Given that we were required to teach off a standard lesson plan document that we created together and have weekly Professional Learning Community (PLC) meetings, our only option was to meet after school or during lunch.

We all got along great, but one teacher was brand new and, let's say, not enjoying her time. We all wanted to support each other positively but were also super busy and if we weren't disciplined, we could lose hours on tangents about challenging students, parents, and teaching in general.

We discovered having a set time and structure for our meetings worked the best. We met once a week during lunch break. Meeting at lunch meant that the meeting had a finite limit. We delegated anything we didn't finish to an "items to finish" document. We also had meeting norms, the first of which was "No longer than five minutes of emotional check-in at the beginning of the meeting." This was necessary if we were to accomplish our goals within 45 minutes. It also helped keep the "venting" to a minimum.

As I discussed in setting boundaries on time, anytime during the week I received a text or email about something non-urgent, I would ask, "Can it wait until our meeting?" Because once that person "stopped by" after school, it would be hard to cut off their stream of venting.

So, I understand that some of this makes me come off as an "ice queen." If you knew me personally, you would realize how funny that is. I talk a big talk, but the reality is that setting boundaries with people is still something I work on. I am highly empathetic and struggle with not "jumping in" immediately to help and fix things for people. Boundaries, again. Many educators are hardwired this same way. If therapeutic language is your thing, go ahead and call it "over- functioning." Over-functioning is unproductive and squanders the emotional energy we need for ourselves. So, like many, I am a work in progress. But becoming aware of our tendencies is the first step to making positive changes.

ONE WAY THAT I FEEL MORE COMFORTABLE CUTTING NEGATIVE people short is to have a repertoire of phrases that I use that are authentic and empathetic but politely extricate myself from extended discussions. I want to validate people. Their experience is real for them. For some people, complaining is just a really bad habit. If they were to question their habit, they would likely recognize that constantly venting makes us feel less empowered and less hopeful. But for the most part, many people are unconscious of the negative radio station they are tuned into. They ARE noticing everything going wrong: every student who is dysregulated, every unreasonable parent, and every staff member who is "offensively cheerful." That's what their satellite is tuned to. I don't want to sound patronizing by saying I feel sad for them, but I empathize. That's a disempowering and miserable way to make your way through life. And to make it worse, I know it contributes to a negative vibe in their classroom, eliciting increased negative behavior from students. It's a vicious circle.

So here are some phrases I use. They feel authentic to me, but if this is different from your voice, then work on some phrasing of your own.

"Gosh, that sounds hard. I hope your day/week gets better. I have to run, but I'll think good thoughts for you!"

"Dang, that's tough. I hope the rest of your day goes smoother. I have to bounce, but I'll say a little prayer to the teaching gods for you!"

"I'm sorry to hear that. I hope the rest of your day gets better!"

"Urg, I hate it when that happens! Good luck, I hope it turns out OK for you!"

It's Not a Competition

Here's what NOT to say. With every good intention in the world, some of us try to show another person that we "get it" and can relate to them by adding our own story. We cut them off. "You think that's bad, wait til you hear this…"

In our mind, we are "bonding" and validating. In their mind, not so much. It can come across as self-centered and wanting to hijack the conversation.

. . .

I USED TO DO THIS OFTEN UNTIL ONE DAY, SOMEONE CALLED ME ON it and told me I wasn't "a good listener." I was astonished. Me? Not a good listener? I learned that to be a good listener, you need to ask questions, not just wait to add a story of your own. That's a topic for another book.

Whenever I feel the urge to add my own story now, I think of a joke that hits painfully close to home. I can't remember who told it, but I do remember wincing when I heard it. Here it is. Dr. Martin Luther King is on a plane, working on his famous speech. The person beside him asks what he is doing and what the speech is about. Dr. King starts to say, "I have a dream," and the person interrupts, saying, I had a dream too and in my dream…" Ouch. You get the point.

HERE'S THE OTHER ISSUE WITH THIS SCENARIO. ADDING YOUR STORY prolongs the conversation. Once we start "trauma sharing," the negative direction of the discourse is off and running like a freight train, and it's hard to stop the momentum. It becomes a competition. We're competing for whose class is the worst behaved and whose parents are the most high-maintenance, who works more, who sleeps less, and who is more stressed. You know the drill. I don't know who should keep score and what the actual prize is, but it feels like a warped competition. And when we step away from that conversation, we are unlikely to feel uplifted and energized. We just participated in draining our own battery.

Go on a Mental Diet Detox

Here's another hill I'll die on, and something I repeat every chance I have. I kept this phrase posted on the front of my desk for 20 years.

"Your mind is the most fertile soil in the universe. Be mindful of what you plant in it." -

Unknown origin.

OUR ULTIMATE GOAL IS TO LEAD A MORE PEACEFUL, LESS STRESSFUL life in which we are less reactive to what's happening inside and outside the classroom.

Einstein said,

"The most important decision anyone has to make is whether they believe they live in a friendly or hostile universe."

I vote for friendly all the way. I want to believe that people are doing the best they can with the skills they have in the situation they find themselves in. I call that extending people's grace.

It's hard to live in a mindset of a friendly universe when what we are planting in our minds is evidence of the opposite.

Most people understand that what we physically consume will have an effect on our bodies and how we feel. For example, if your basic diet were to binge all day on junk food, fizzy drinks, alcohol, or drugs, you would understand that it would hurt your body, and you wouldn't be performing at your peak. However, not everyone makes the same connection with what they are consuming mentally and how they are feeling and acting. Treats such as wine, cocktails, chocolate, and funnel cakes are fine and delicious on a limited basis, but they shouldn't comprise the foundation of your diet. And it's the same with what we "mentally" consume.

IN THE COMPANION WORKBOOK, YOU WILL FIND A SIMPLE EXERCISE to help you identify and evaluate the bulk of your mental diet in the following areas: books, TV shows, films, podcasts, social media habits, and your relationship to the 24-hour new cycle.

THE EXERCISE WILL ASK YOU TO LIST SPECIFIC THINGS IN EACH category and evaluate whether they support your view of living in a friendly or hostile universe. For example, suppose you only listen to podcasts about True Crime and solving murders. In that case, you should seek balance with more positive topics such as personal growth, inspiration, or stories about what is going right in the world. Sure, these might not be on the top podcast charts, but you can find them with some digging. Let me not waste this opportunity to suggest that listening to my podcast, *Teacher Self-Care and Life Balance*, could be a great place to start.

YOU GET THE IDEA. YOU WANT TO EVALUATE THE SOCIAL MEDIA accounts you follow - are they all about snarky teacher memes, #teacherquittok, and being enraged at people with a different worldview than yourself? Do you find yourself sucked into a rabbit hole of doom scrolling every time you log on to a social media account "just for a minute?"

In simple terms, does losing time on social media make you feel better or worse about your life, the world? What about the constant barrage of ads adverts subliminally suggesting you are deficient? The message is that you are not good enough as you are. You need better clothes, hair, make-up, you need to be skinnier, bulkier, you need to be healthier ("buy these supplements and medications to help").

A Quick Word About the News Cycle

The world needs informed and inspired individuals to take action against injustice as they see it worldwide. If you're an activist, I salute you. Keep streaming the news.

But for many people, constantly streaming the news cycle causes their nervous system to be on constant high alert. The news cycle is designed to keep reporting the worst horrors happening on repeat until something else bad happens. It is the epitome of training our subconscious mind to perceive the world is hostile and dangerous.

Back in the days of hunter-gatherer communities, our nervous system was designed to go into fight-or-flight mode when danger was imminent. That danger could have been an intruder, an attacking animal, or a natural disaster in the immediate vicinity.

Even before the advent of travel and communication, we lived in small communities without knowing what was happening beyond even a few miles of us. Our Brain and nervous system have not evolved sufficiently to comfortably take in every bad thing happening in the world without it negatively affecting us. As famous psychologist Dr. Daniel Amen says, watching the news cycle on repeat is like "drinking trauma from a fire hose." It's simply too much for us to handle.

Even as recently as 20 - 30 years ago, I remember getting the news once a day from a paper delivered to my doorstep, sometimes twice a day if I turned on the TV for the 6:00 PM news. Now, breaking news streams 24/7 on television and radio, inserts itself on social media feeds, and it's increasingly harder to limit our exposure to all the trauma. Proactively limiting our exposure to the news is one of the best things we can do from a mental diet standpoint. It also helps to remember that the friendly, good stuff happening in the world does not sell newspapers.

Summary

To protect our mental and emotional well-being, we need to be proactive about limiting our exposure to toxically negative people, even if we need to work with them daily. Validating people's experiences and being empathetic is important. Still, we need to learn strategies and scripts to avoid getting dragged into a negative spiral and participating in a cycle of "competitive misery" about whose situation is worse. Structured meetings and positive routines can help. Additionally, maintaining a balanced "mental diet" by reducing exposure to negative media and consuming positive content is crucial to ensuring our nervous system isn't living in a constant state of high alert.

Get Empowered

Ways to Practice This Mindset Habit Starting Today

1 Recognize that proactively protecting our peace is private work. There is no need to start reposting memes about cutting toxic people out of our lives on social media. There is no need to let people know you think they are toxic. Quietly unsubscribe, unfollow, or unfriend without causing any drama. Making a big

deal about withdrawing your attention from toxically negative things is the antithesis of protecting your peace.

2 BE THE TEACHER WHO STOPS THE "TRAUMA SHARING" CYCLE IN the staff room. Before you walk in or know you will pass other teachers, think of the best thing in your classroom that day. Think of something positive you can share about a student, your class, a parent, or another staff member. Once you've set your satellite to "The Good Stuff" channel, you'll find that there are plenty of positive things worth sharing.

3 CAUTION: READ THE TONE IN THE STAFF ROOM FIRST. IF THERE IS a negative vibe, heat your lunch and be on your way. Some people may find your cheerfulness "offensive." If your staff room is constantly negative regardless of your efforts, then having a lunch date with your teacher best friend in your room or a walk-and-talk lunch once a week would be a better solution for you. As the saying goes, "Better to be alone than to be in bad company."

4 BE STRATEGIC WHEN SCHEDULING GRADE-SPAN OR TEAM meetings. Try to schedule them during school hours so that they do not drag on indefinitely and leave room for people to "vent" for a long time. Set meeting norms that include items such as "focus on solutions."

5 MAKE A LIST OF NATURAL PHRASES YOU CAN SAY TO MAKE PEOPLE feel seen, heard, and validated. These phrases will also enable you to extricate yourself from complaining sessions politely. Practice

them until they don't feel awkward. As I like to say, validate the person and then bounce.

6 COMPLETE THE INVENTORY OF YOUR MEDIA CONSUMPTION exercise in the Workbook. A similar exercise was in *Positive Mindset Habits for Teachers*. If you have done it before, update it and compare the two lists. Have you made positive changes? Or is your idea of "relaxing" binge-watching or binge-listening to true crime stories? Challenge yourself to take a break from the trauma for a week and see if your mood and outlook feel any different.

10

Coming Full Circle

So there you have it. My outline for this book included several more chapters, but again, less is more. I didn't want to risk wasting another year fretting over them and this (also awkward) conclusion. The call for you to make some positive changes and the need to provide you with the tools are too great.

THIS BOOK HAS MANY STRATEGIES TO GET YOU STARTED ON YOUR journey to a more empowered experience as an educator. Reminding you of my advice from the beginning chapters of this book and how I've approached professional development for years, I encourage you to "take what you need and leave the rest."

Find the tools that appeal to you and could make the most impact, and start there. This book was set up in as much of a logical sequence as I could provide. However, all of these concepts are interconnected. If you know your most urgent issue is that you say "yes" way too often when you really want to say "no," open the book to that section and get to work.

For those of you more comfortable following a logical path (I salute you!)

Here's Your Essential Roadmap:

1 Decide what is most critical to you and your students what you want to accomplish in education. This will be your North Star.

2 Next, recognize that your worth in this world is intrinsic and not tied to your identity as an educator. Doing so will help you keep things in perspective when things are overwhelmingly stressful (and they will be at times).

3 Work on being less reactive and more proactive. You embody empowerment when you put your energy into things you can control. Be so busy focusing on things you can impact that you have less time to worry about things beyond your control.

4 Move beyond the idea that one day things in your life will be perfectly balanced. They won't. Use the tools provided to help you gain clarity about priorities and make intentional choices about which responsibilities you will juggle and which you will let go. Make peace with the idea that not everything will get done.

5 Now that you have given yourself permission to do less, perfect the art of declining requests with confidence, professionalism, and a student-focused reason.

6 Be mindful of limiting beliefs and "stories" you tell yourself that are not resourceful and are at odds with your desire to feel more in control of your experience. Use the tools provided to help uncover these, then rewrite the narrative you tell yourself.

7 Finally, recognize that being overly stressed, exhausted and emotionally depleted is not just a function of your schedule and

having too many tasks to accomplish. To feel more in control of your time and energy, you must proactively protect your peace from people who drain you. Become skilled in setting healthy boundaries and validating people without getting sucked into their drama.

Gently Now - Setting Yourself Up for Success

I don't know if this is the first personal development book you have ever read or the hundredth. It seems every other TikTok or podcast these days focuses on "how to handle your life better," so it's unlikely that this book will shake you to your core like my Steven Covey experience did thirty years ago. But even if this isn't your first time at the personal development rodeo, here are some gentle reminders to set you up for success.

FIRST, CONSISTENT HABITS CAN POWERFULLY CHANGE YOUR LIFE; isolated mini-events, not so much. Just like completing one sit-up won't lead to six-pack abs, don't expect to use one of these tools one time and transform your entire experience. You have been functioning in a way you have been conditioned to and in a way that is likely comfortable to you and those around you. Deciding to do things differently will take commitment to a new way of thinking, not just a new way of doing. It will take time to make using these tools a habit and your normal way of operating within the school system. Venturing out might be a little uncomfortable initially, but I promise you the destination will be worth it.

NEXT, TREAD GENTLY WITH OTHERS AND WITH YOURSELF. IF YOU move forward with the idea that setting healthy boundaries and protecting yourself from burnout, resentment, and exhaustion is a positive thing that benefits everyone in your life, things will go more smoothly. Sure, new habits take time and often take us right out of our comfort zone. But what you've been doing until now hasn't been working, or you wouldn't have found your way to this book. Your first attempts at setting boundaries or letting a ball intentionally drop will feel uncomfortable. You might not do either with as much grace as you hoped.

START WITH SMALLER, LOWER-STAKES ISSUES. REMEMBER, YOU HAVE to walk before you learn to run. Even crawling will be a step in the right direction. Start with some small "wins" to gain your confidence. Don't tackle the greatest boundary bully or try to ditch your most significant extracurricular responsibility immediately. Try setting a lower-stakes boundary with a pushy parent or overbearing colleague before you try to tackle your administrator. Gain confidence, celebrate the small wins, and before too long, protecting your time and energy will start to feel like second nature. Once you realize how much smoother life goes when you start using these tools and feel more in control of your experience, you will be hooked.

FINALLY, DON'T JUDGE A BOOK BY ITS TONE. MY CASUAL APPROACH to writing is not everyone's cup of tea. I write the types of books I would have appreciated as a teacher. While my tone is casual, my commitment to research is anything but. As well as being backed by science, the concepts and ideas in this book have been tested by me and other teachers I coach. The results have been positive and impactful.

. . .

ANY PHYSICIST WILL TELL YOU THAT WE LIVE IN AN INTERACTIVE universe: it is proven science that physical forces respond to how we think and act and the outcomes we expect. Please don't write off what I have presented as naively idealistic just because my tone offends. You can learn from me, even if you are annoyed that I'm unconcerned about split infinitives and ending sentences with prepositions. I'm less concerned with syntax and more concerned about helping you get results.

HERE'S MY FINAL ADVICE: PLEASE DON'T DENY YOURSELF THE possibility of positive change by arguing for your limitations before you even get going. "That would never work with my admin!" "You don't understand, things in my district are different!" are all excuses to talk ourselves out of trying something that scares us. Trust me, I've been guilty of these thoughts and more. Confidence comes from results. Results only happen if you try. If you try and win, well ... you won. If you try and fail, you get feedback. You'll know how to approach things differently next time.

COMING FULL CIRCLE FROM MY AWKWARD INTRODUCTION, HERE'S the plea again: evolve and learn these new skills or risk burning out in a career you learned to be a victim of. Use these tools. Risk getting a little messy. Discover things about yourself.

DON'T BEAT YOURSELF UP FOR NOT INVESTING IN LEARNING THESE skills sooner in your career. That was then; this is now.

As the great Maya Angelou said,

 "When you know better, do better."

I leave you with this. I believe in you and your ability to create a more positive experience in education. The world needs your time and talents inside the classroom and beyond. You **can** choose to walk down a different street.

Thanks for trusting me to show you how.

Epilogue

Poem by Portia Nelson, *There's a Hole in My Sidewalk: The Romance of Self-Discovery*

Chapter One of My Life.

I walk down the street. There's a deep hole in the sidewalk. I fall in.

I am lost. I am helpless. It isn't my fault. It takes forever to find a way out.

Chapter Two.

I walk down the same street. There's a deep hole in the sidewalk. I pretend I don't see it. I fall in again. I can't believe I'm in the same place! But it isn't my fault. And it still takes a long time to get out.

Chapter Three.

I walk down the same street. There's a deep hole in the sidewalk. I see it there. I still fall in. It's a habit! My eyes are open. I know where I am. It is my fault. I get out immediately.

Chapter Four.

I walk down the same street. There's a deep hole in the sidewalk. I walk around it.

Chapter Five.

I walk down a different street."

Good Karma Request

Thank you for taking time to read this book. I truly hope you feel encouraged and empowered to start using these tools.

I have a request. The indie publishing space is drowning in AI-generated books. It's very hard for anyone without a huge marketing budget to get their message out there.

Two easy ways that would help other teachers find their way to this book would be:

1. Tell a colleague about it. Heck, tell your administrator. Along with the Companion Workbook, this resource is a very low cost option for a campus wide book study.

2. Leave a short review on Amazon or Goodreads. It doesn't need to be an essay, just a sentence or two or even just a rating. This truly helps the book be found.

Doing either or both of these things would mean the work to me. Thank you!

Good Karma Request

Again, thank you for all that you do in the world of education. It is a tough job, for sure. When things are going well, it's so rewarding and can feel like the best job in the world. Don't give up hope! I wish you many more joyful days in your career.

Grace

Need More?

If this book is your first time visiting with me, good news! There are plenty of ways to interact me.

Check out zero-cost weekly content from me via my podcast. You can listen on any of your favorite podcast players.

For information on self-study courses or courses with coaching you can visit: www.gracestevens.com

Need More?

I am available for professional development, keynote speeches and author Q & As via Zoom (or equivalent) or in-person if you happen to be in Northern California.

I am not great at social media (intentionally!) but feel free to reach out to me via email at grace@gracestevens.com

About the Author

A former corporate girl, Grace quit VP life to pursue her dream job as a public school teacher in 2002. After 20 years in the classroom, she now focuses full-time on helping educators have a more positive teaching experience.

Grace combines her signature mantra, "Your energy teaches more than your lesson plans," with two decades of study in behavioral therapy, positive psychology, and NLP to create science-based habits for overwhelmed educators.

She is the author of several books including the best-selling _Positive Mindset Habits for Teachers_ and hosts the *Teacher Self-Care and Life Balance* podcast.

Also by Grace Stevens

For information about self -study courses on these books please visit:

www.gracestevens.com/courses

www.ingramcontent.com/pod-product-compliance
Lightning Source LLC
Chambersburg PA
CBHW070604010526
44118CB00012B/1443